Praise Those Str

"*I thought that I was destined*
forever, I had tried everything ... *... was at my*
lowest point when a friend introduced me to Lesley, and I thank
my lucky stars that they did! Lesley knew exactly how to pull me
out of the dark hole I was in, and ever since that day, the light
at the end of the tunnel has gotten brighter, bolder and
stronger. I smile an authentic smile, I laugh a proper belly laugh
and I say I love you and mean it. I have found my new path,
and it is laced with happy memories, smiles and giddy moments
of joy. Never give up hope, there is always a fairy godmother
waiting for you somewhere, I found mine in Lesley!"
Samantha - The Goddess Lifestyle Programme

"*Since finding Lesley, my life has taken a huge U-Turn, and so*
has my attitude. I use to weigh myself every morning and spend
the rest of the day starving myself to get the next result. I would
crash and burn, binge and purge and I hated myself. I would
look in the mirror and turn away in disgust. Lesley taught me
how to love myself, how to respect myself and more importantly
how to love my perfect imperfections. I owe so much to Lesley
and the Goddess Club programmes, and cannot recommend
them enough!"
Louisa - G2 Programme & The Goddess Lifestyle Programme

"*Everyday is a blessing, every smile is a joy and every moment*
that I think of myself, I know I am winning! There is no more
hurt, no more pain and no more soul-destroying efforts to fail at.
I haven't been on a diet for over a year, and I feel the best I
have ever felt. Thanks to Lesley and her online coaching and her
books, I am born again and I AM HAPPY!!"
Jennifer - The Success Diary & The Goddess Lifestyle Programme

"I am the biggest skeptic around, and when a friend started telling me about this programme she was doing, I thought - yeah, just another b****** thing that wont work. But then my friend started to change, I don't even know what changed about her, but I could see how happy she was becoming, how she was dressing differently and how she seemed more confident. I had to get in on this wonderful magical diet or plan that she had found, and when she introduced me to The Goddess Club, I still had my reservations, but Lesley was incredible. She rang me, talked to me, never once pushed me or sold to me. She left the game in play for me, at my pace, in my time and I bit.
The crazy thing is, the programme only bloody works! I feel amazing, love love love it! Literally, I am spilling love everywhere! Amazing! Thanks Lesley!"
Angela - The Goddess Lifestyle Programme

"I can only say Thank you from the bottom of my heart to Lesley. What I have learnt about myself and my body since starting this journey of self exploration has been remarkable, I have fallen in love, I have found love and I can give love willingly. My life is the happiest it has ever been, and me.... Well.... Happiness doesn't say enough, I am over the moon with how my life is! Thank you Lesley!"
Janet - The Goddess Lifestyle Programme

"I never thought I could feel so special, I truly do feel like a Goddess! Thank you Lesley!"
Sarah - The G2 & The Goddess Lifestyle Programme

"Life is wonderful! I am a Goddess! And to all of my fellow goddesses, I love you all!"
Melissa - The Goddess Lifestyle Programme

"It really is all about me! I am important, I do matter and I am worth it! Ladies, never feel as though you are alone or struggling a different battle. Lesley has shown me that we are all fighting internal demons, but the answers lie in finding peace and loving yourself!"
Bridget - THe Goddess Lifestyle Programme

The Sugar Coated Secret Love Affair

The Sugar Coated Secret Love Affair

Learning to Love Yourself, Your Body, Your Food and Your Life!

Lesley Morrison

To my incredible partner who stands by me, no matter what
crazy, whacky and mind-boggling ideas I come up with!
To my amazing mum, who is the best mother in the world!
And to my dog, who is just so damn cute!

Contents

We Are At War - My Story	9
What Was Missing?	18
The Dieting Lifestyle	24
A New Leaf	30
A Sugar Coated Secret Love Affair	35
Listen Up and Pay Attention	45
The Exciting New Relationship	53
Up Down Up Down Up Down	58
Friend, Foe or Frenemy?	62
The True Transformation	72
Our Own "Ism's"	78
You Are Not To Blame	85
What If There Was no Wagon?	91
Where Is Home?	96
Know Who You Are	100
Are We There Yet?	106
Macros This! Calories That! WTF?	116
The Computer Says No!	122
Scrutiny Mutiny	130
A Declaration of Love	136
Let's Make Up And Be Friends	138
Find Your Reason	144
Be Reborn	149
Create Your Own Future	151
Who Said That? (Binge Bitch, Binge)	153
Tell Your Tale	157
Copy Cats	160
The Real Stories	164
Softly Softly	168
FUD	173
Haters Gonna Hate	175
Sorority Solidarity	179
Feelings Don't Lie	183
Food-ism	188
F#!k Rules	192
Forgive and Forget	193
Find The Passion in The Pans	196
Give Yourself A Hug	202
Let Love Light The Way	205
Your Dream Body	210
The Spiritual Sanctity of Self-Love	214
Only Do It If You Love It	216
Embrace Yourself	217

Your Body is Precious.
It is our vehicle for
awakening.

Buddha

We Are At War - My Story

We are all at war, and more shockingly, we are all at war with the same thing - our body.

Truth is, we all want smaller, slimmer, bigger, better, faster, stronger - we all want something. We all want to feel happier with our body, we all want to feel more confident in our own skin!

We all want to be and feel HAPPY!
We all want freedom!

So, are we actually at war with our body - or are we at war with what we put in to our body?
Deeper still, are we at war with what we put into our body - or are we at war with what goes on inside our own minds, our own thoughts, perceptions and beliefs?

We are all at war with something, and more shockingly - we are all at war with the same thing!
But it isn't really our body!

_____

Have you ever been out at the supermarket, doing your food shopping and seen another woman filling her basket with vegetables, nuts, fruits - seemingly healthy foods. Have you ever seen this woman and thought:
"I wish I could be more like her - I bet she has the perfect life!"?

Or maybe you have been out with friends, having a bite to eat at a restaurant, and a friend has ordered a skinny salad with no dressing - and you thought "Wow, she is so dedicated, I wish I could be more like her!"?

Perhaps whilst out clothes shopping you see a complete stranger browsing the swimwear, or those gorgeous low slung backless summer dresses, and you have thought: "I wish I could wear those clothes, and dress like her!".

I wish, I wish, I wish!

We are all at war with something - but what is it?

I can tell you that the woman buying the vegetables is craving chocolate, pizzas, burgers, breads, sweets, cakes - she is not happy!
She is living under the countless rules and restrictions of the newest and latest diet craze - she is not at war with her body!
She is at war with her mind, her own need to be controlled by the fear of gaining a pound or not losing another!
She is NOT happy!

The friend ordering the skinny salad with no dressing - she is not happy!
She is watching everyone enjoy their food as she eats yet another salad. She is living a life of restraint and discipline, likely topped with a hint of resentment.
She is in control of the out of control need to track every calorie that is stopping her from having fun and enjoying the company of her friends.
She is not at war with her body, she is at war with her own need to be controlled by the anxiety of not being perfect or not reaching her goal!
She is NOT happy!

The lady looking at the swimwear and low slung backless summer dresses is living a life of forced external confidence - held at ransom by what other expect of her - She is not happy!

Those dresses may forever hang on her clothes rail never to be worn, and she may never have the self confidence to wear the swimwear - in fact she probably wishes that she could wear them too!

But she is not at war with her body, she is fighting against the expectations of her own confidence. She may look strong and fearless on the outside, but on the inside she is at war with her own beliefs, expectations and judgements - fighting a forever repeating battle of up and down days.

She is NOT happy!

We are ALL at war with something!

When we see these women out and about, living their lives, buying their groceries, eating out with friends or clothes shopping, we only see the outside story, our own perceptions of these people.

In essence, we make up their story!

We judge the book by its cover!

It is a bit like an instagram filter, we do not see "behind the scenes" or the "real story".

We do not see them bingeing on chocolate, crying over a glass of wine, hiding under the duvet wishing that the world would go away, just for a few hours.

We do not see them obsessively tracking their calories, stepping on the scales daily or looking in the mirror pinching their fat rolls and turning away in disgust.

We do not see the truth!

Only what we perceive to be the truth!

You may be wandering how I know all of this?

Because, I was one of those women too!

I was one of those - I'll just have the skinny salad! I'll buy that dress, but never wear it! I'll fill my basket with fruit and vegetables!
I was **NOT** happy!

You probably don't know me, and even if you have met me, the truth is, you probably still do not know the real me.
The barriers that I had surrounding me for such a long time were impenetrable, I was a fortress of "fuck you" for a really long time.
I was not happy!

Why?

Expectations!!!
The pressure to be and feel perfect!!!

To never put a foot wrong or make a mistake or gain a pound or drink alcohol or eat a burger or have a take away or heavens forbid, eat some cake! I was a prisoner of my own beliefs and expectations.

I was a personal trainer you see, and my problem wasn't with what others expected of me, but my own expectations of what others expected of me.

A vicious cycle of my own beliefs!

I would put so much pressure on myself, I spent more time thinking about what others thought of me, that I felt like I had to portray the perfect life!

I ate vegetables, you know all of those superfoods like arugula, kale, bok choi and lentils. I certainly didn't drink, smoke, stay out late, eat take aways, cakes or crisps. I spent hours every day in the gym perfecting my already perfectly sculpted body, trying to take off another pound, look a little leaner, to kick ass a little more.

This is what I THOUGHT people expected of me! This is what I thought I had to do.

The more I thought this way, the more I rebelled against it.
The more pressure I put on myself, the more I fought back.
The more I believed this was what people expected, the more I stared in the mirror and hated the imperfections looking back at me!
I was NOT happy!

I felt like a fake and a failure and I started to hate my work, I started to feel resentment and with that, I fought back even more!

I battled my own demons with food, and would have epic highs with epic lows. One week I would only eat chicken and salad, followed closely by a revolt, bingeing on Chinese take away, fried chicken, beer and cake until I felt sick. Followed by the oh-so-familiar "I'll start again on Monday", (because diets always start on Monday, right?)

I started to get ill, my body was fighting back against me and I couldn't defend myself against simple bugs, colds, flus.
My health wasn't what it once was and this just exacerbated the problem!

Fuck you body! Fuck you for gaining 10lbs, for getting sick, for being tired. FOR LETTING ME DOWN!

This cycle of self-hate continued for years!

Up, down, left, right, round and round!
One day to the next!

Then I started skipping meals altogether, fuelling myself with coffee, energy drinks and sugar free fizzy drinks.

Soon after came *"yay, it's Friday! Let's drink until we cant feel anymore!"*
Because that always helps…. right?

I was that slim lady buying vegetables living under constant rules; rules that made me rebel.

I was that lady ordering the skinny salad with no dressing, living under the scrutiny of my own beliefs of what others expected of me; beliefs that made me fight back.

I was that lady buying low slung summer dresses and swimwear, giving off an aura of confidence and fearlessness, and yes, those dresses hung on my clothes rail for years, never worn, because on the inside, I hated my body!

Until one relatively normal day in my life, a small amount of pain started in my right hip, a day later, I was limping, I could barely stand.
Within 24 hours I had a full on fever, sweats, shivers, no appetite, no energy and agonising pain radiating throughout my right leg and torso.

I went to bed thinking it was just another bad case of flu, but it wasn't!

That night I was rushed into hospital and pumped full of antibiotics and pain killers.

The next day I was rushed to surgery for a suspected ruptured appendix.

The surgery went reasonably well, but it was anything but routine. My appendix was intact, healthy and left alone. BUT, my ovaries, womb and fallopian tubes were not.

My organs were so inflamed, that they had pushed organs into other organs. I had a blocked fallopian tube, and later on, during a secondary surgery, I found out that I had endometriosis, that I would never be able to have children, at least not naturally, and probably not even with medical assistance either.

I was told that if I hadn't have been admitted that night my story, well, my story may not be very long.

I had scarring on my liver where the other organs had been pushing against it, and a life long disease that is incurable - and in that very moment, I knew I needed to start listening to my body and looking after it.

But it wasn't going to be easy!

I played a game of chicken with the grim reaper that day, and luckily for me, I won.

Luckily for my body, I learnt something that changed the rest of my life!

We are not being judged and expected of by others, we are just here to live our best lives and love our selves best.

You see, we are all at war with something - but it is not our bodies, and not even with our food.

We are actually all at war with our own minds, our own expectations and our own beliefs!

You only get one life, and one body to live it from within.
Make it the best you can!

What Was Missing?

When I look back at this time of my life, I realise a lot, I realise how much shit I have put my body through.
I see how I have never stopped to actually care for, love or listen to my body.
I understand that I treated my body like dirt, and in return, she couldn't look after me and I now know that my body is my absolute best friend, my rock, my pillar of strength and the one thing that I need more than anything, in order to lead my best and truest life.

My body, well, she is my hero!

She fights back with grit and determination, despite all of the crap that I have thrown at her... and all I ever needed to do was to actually sit back and listen to her for a minute.

Hear her cries, her wishes, her wants.
See her scars, her strengths and her perfect imperfections.
Respect her!
Love her!
Worship her!

And, once I did this, in return, she would look after me, love me and give me the best possible life.

So what was missing back then that could have change everything?

LOVE!

Pure, unbreakable, beautiful, deep, connected and spiritual LOVE!
Not for another person or thing, but for my self, my body, my being!

I had to put everything together, like a giant puzzle of life, so I spent a lot of time studying the human mind. Learning about psychology, mindset, mindfulness and neurosciences.
Luckily, this all fascinated me!

I started to connect the dots, and complete what seemed like a massive paint by numbers of my life, but as I did this, it was like the small window that I had been looking out at life through, suddenly opened up into a huge panoramic viewing window.

The world and everything in it suddenly became vivid, colourful, beautiful.

Things that I had never noticed before were suddenly amazing to see. Even silly things like the sound butterfly wings make as they fly past you (yep they make a sound), or the beauty of a flower opening up for the first time in spring. Taking the window seat on a plane and looking out over the breath taking views from above, hearing the waves crashing against the shore, the birds singing in the morning or the pollen that bees collect on their legs.

All of these things had passed me by until I opened up my own heart to myself and my body.

You see, when you start to feel love for yourself, you start to see, hear, feel and experience the world in a very different, much more exciting and grateful way.

The world becomes bigger, but somehow you see and hear more of it.
Your senses are heightened and your life is enriched.

But more so, and more importantly, when you start to feel love for yourself and your body, you start to hear your own self much more clearly.

It's a bit like, oh dear, I am going to show my age a little here, remember the old TV sets where you had to tune into the channel using the dial?
It's a bit like that!
You can see the picture behind the static, then all of a sudden you have full technicolour, Hi-Def, 4K clarity in surround sound with sensory perception in wide screen.

You hear your body, and in doing so, you feel more and give more back.
You start to take notice!

————————————

As a personal trainer, I would hear a lot of my female clients talking about bloating, lethargy, digestive issues, IBS, diarrhoea, constipation, period pains, stomach cramps, headaches, joint aches and a long list of frustrating and sometimes incapacitating problems.

I noticed how everything was always negative, down beat and bad news.

But why do we focus on the lows so much?

Well, it is because this is the only time we really listen, or should I say *"hear"* our own body.
We only notice when there is something to complain about.

Think about it! Take a moment now....

If you are noticing anything about your body right now, whilst reading this - I can almost guarantee that it is negative.
It is pain!
It is discomfort.
You don't like it!
But... what are you doing to remedy it?

Why cant we see the highs as well?
Why can't we hear what the body is saying to us?

Take something that we all get, period pains for example!
Yes, they can be uncomfortable, inconvenient, frustrating, BUT as women, most of us are blessed with the absolutely amazing ability to bear children, and if it wasn't for these little monthly gifts from mother nature, well, that wouldn't be possible.

Gaia has entrusted us beautiful women with the biggest responsibility know to human kind!
The creation and nurturing of a new life!
Surely that is a blessing!

But what about something more mundane, like bloating?

This is another extremely common complaint.
But rather than allowing it to control you and your life, why not listen to your body, what is she telling you?

If you listen up, she is letting you know that you have consumed something that she doesn't like or maybe cannot process.

Rather than ignoring the symptom, try and establish the cause, so that you don't have to keep feeling this way.

Your body does not have the power of speech, she cannot use words to communicate with you, but she is ALWAYS telling you something.
You just need to sit up and pay attention.

We all deserve love and happiness, but in order to find these things, we really need to start loving ourselves first.

And believe me, you will not find love or happiness in a weight or a dress size.
Love comes from within, and cannot be forced or faked.

In order to find true happiness, you need to open up your mind, alter your perceptions and step away from the rules and restrictions that you have been living by.

You need to alter your mindset and find your beauty, confidence and smile from within your own mind.
You need to start listening to your body and what she is telling you, and in doing so help her to feel loved, nurtured, and strong like a treasured friend, like a true goddess.

You yourself, as much as anybody in the entire universe, deserve your love and affection.

Buddha

The Dieting Lifestyle

We have all been there, right?

I'll start on Monday!
Diets always start on Monday....
Why is that?
What is so great about Mondays?

Whether you have tried to cut your carbs, reduce your fat, lower your sugar, count calories, track your macros or kept within your points, we have ALL dieted at some point.
And we all know many other women who are trying to do the same.
But why do we feel the need to succumb to this crazy culture of cray-cray diets?

And more importantly, why do we keep doing the same thing over and over again, thinking that this time it will be different?
This time it'll work!
This time I will stick to it!

And what is a diet anyway?
What does the word even mean?

The word "diet" didn't appear in the English language until the 13th century, and originated from the Greek work "diaita" (δiαiτα), which actually meant *way of life*.

But regardless of where the word came from or what it means, there is no single diet that provides you with a lifestyle that you can sustain forever.
And to diet forever, well, thats not a fun way of life, surely?

You can't count calories forever, resist temptations forever, avoid sugar forever, track macros forever.

Diets have become like a full time job, they are taking up so much of our precious time and energy, and we see very minimal long-term rewards or results.
I mean, is that the kind of unfulfilling "dead-end" job that you would like to have?

They bind you to rules, restrictions, routines and restraints that lead to you feeling as though you are living a life of deprivation, control and well, lets be honest... failure! That's NO fun!

Diets are doomed to fail!

I remember when I tried to drop a few pounds before a holiday, I decided to do the low carb diet.
I felt great for about three days, then I got the dreaded carb flu and it took every ounce of my own self-control not to dive head first into a tub of Neapolitan ice cream... why I even wanted that I will never know... I don't even like ice cream. I felt like I had won the war when I didn't cave, but then I started feeling light headed, dizzy and nauseous. Eventually, I had to give in... and damn, did I give in spectacularly!

My point is, the hurdles that you face, the restrictions that you have to live with and the strength and discipline required to stay within the rules, are way beyond what most people can realistically achieve.
No matter how strong willed you may be!

In fact, long term, most diets actually have more health risks than benefits, including depriving you and your body of some really crucial & amazing nutrients and vital nourishment!

We've all been there, we've all deprived ourselves and we have all cracked under the pressure, so wouldn't it be an amazing feeling to live free from rules, restrictions, meal planning, deprivation, cravings, guilt and all of the other emotions that come tied to a "diet"?

In fact, wouldn't it be nice to be able to go out for a meal with your friends and just order whatever the hell you wanted.... WITHOUT feeling as though you have failed again, let yourself down or just lost control and binged on everything in sight?

Deprivation leads to bingeing!
Bingeing leads to guilt!
Guilt leads to self loathing!
Self loathing leads to more bingeing!
Before you know it you are in a very vicious cycle of
Eat ~ Sleep ~ Weigh ~ Repeat!

Does that sound like the kind of lifestyle that you want to be a part of forever?

HELL NO! I don't think so, thank you very much!
Where is the fun, the smiles, the love and the happiness... Oh yeah, it has been sucked out by all of these rules that I MUST live by!

_____

The diet industry wants you to believe that their diet is the best thing since sliced bread and instant noodles. They know what they are doing and how to market to your weaknesses, your pains, your vulnerabilities.
They know how to suck you in, chew you up and then spit you back out 6 months later without having achieved a thing... other than the feeling that you have failed AGAIN!

How shitty is that?

But that is why the industry makes so much money, they know it wont work!
They know you wont achieve your goals!
They know you will feel hurt, disappointed, upset and a bit crap, and they know that you will come back again in a few months to try again.

They know that diets do not work!

And believe me, it isn't you!
It isn't your lack of determination, desire, will, strength or belief that makes you fall off of the wagon.

No! It is not YOU! You are NOT broken!

It is the RULES!
It is the RESTRICTIONS!
It is the UN-SUSTAINABILITY!
It is the EXPECTATIONS!
It is THE DIETS!
They are the broken ones!

You could have all of the will in the world, but you can't make something work if it has been designed to make you fail!

So stop blaming yourself and remember...

DIETS DO NOT WORK!!!

I asked some of my clients and friends what the word "*diet*" made them feel, what it meant to them.
These were just a few of the responses that I received:

• Controlled

- Restricted
- Pressure
- Imperfect
- Not good enough
- Calories
- Self Loathing
- Depressed
- Binge Eating
- Out of Control
- Starvation
- Failure
- Monday
- Weak
- Skinny
- Jealous
- Rules
- Deprived
- Tracking
- No Life
- Prisoner
- Hungry
- Fat

Now, I don't want to try and guide you on how you might think or feel, but none of these words paint a very positive picture in my mind.
There is no loving, caring, happy or joyful words here, and they certainly do not sound like a fun, fulfilling and happy lifestyle. Do they?

How many of these feelings/thoughts have you experienced whilst "dieting"?

No amount of salads or squats can make you love your body. That is the work that you need to do in your own mind.

A New Leaf

Over the years, I have come to realise something which I really wish I had stumbled upon a very LONG time ago.

We all want to achieve something, but it isn't weight loss or the perfect size 10.
It isn't six-pack abs or a sculpted set of thighs.
It isn't a certain weight on the scales or an inch loss.

No!

What we want, what we ALL truly want is to just feel happy, confident, free and healthy in our own body!

Believe me, a perfect size 10 or toned abs isn't going to change your mindset, nor is it going to guarantee your happiness.

In some cases, it can actually be quite the opposite. Again, I know this, because I have been there!

I was rapidly approaching a dress size of 14, I had curves, and bumps, and bulges and rolls.
Clothes were tight and comments were being made.
I remember, before I became a personal trainer, an old manager saying to me *"You are piling it on a bit, fatty!"*

No one had ever made this kind of comment to me before, and wow, it really hurt!

I got back down to a size 10, but I still wasn't happy, so I kept going until I was a size 8, then a 6 and then back to an 8, then back down to a 6, then up to a 10…

I dieted! I failed! I binged! I cried!

Achieving my goals didn't cure the problem, which was now inside of my head! *"Fatty!"*

This constant up and down of body weight and size, and the irregularity of my eating patterns never once gave me any satisfaction or happiness.

In fact, now I am happily somewhere between a size 10 and 12, I am the heaviest that I have ever been and there are parts of my body that may not look perfect, but I am happy and this happiness transcends my entire body, mind, spirit, soul and life.
I know that I am healthy, fit, strong and sexy... on the inside and out!

I feel confident walking on the beach in a bikini.
I feel great strutting out in one of the low back dresses that sat on my clothes rail for years. And it feels great to eat what I want.
But none of this came as the result of a diet!
It all came from within my own mind.

———————————

Diets have removed one thing from food that we all need to rediscover - joy!
Food is an amazing thing, not just because of what it is, but what it does for our bodies... the nourishment that it provides, the tastes, smells, textures and combinations.
Food is truly amazing!

Food should be enjoyed, savoured and loved, but instead, food has become the "destroyer" of happiness, the necessary evil that causes us to dislike and disconnect from our own body.

We care so little about our food and ourselves these days, that we rarely spare a thought for what we are putting in, as long as it fits the calories.

We eat subconsciously, we binge in secret, we lie to ourselves and live in denial.

"If I don't admit to it, it never happened!"
"No one will ever know!"
"I can't remember what I had yesterday!"

This needs to change!

You need to find the joy in the nourishment that food gives to you, find love for all of it's healing properties and nutrients. Find pleasure in its tastes, smells and textures!

You need to slow down and start enjoying food!

You need to repair the relationship that you have with food!

Listen to your body!
Listen to your hunger and fullness cues!
Listen to what your body is telling you!
Listen to your tastebuds singing and your tummy thanking you!

Hear your body!

_____

Ask yourself - how much is your body worth to you?
Is it worth more than your car?
Your house?
Your designer handbags or sparkly jewels?

Ask yourself - how much you would enjoy your life if your body started to let you down?
How much do you NEED your body?

Your body is your home, your vessel of transport, your sanctuary, your best friend!

Start thinking of her with higher value, with a greater respect and consider her needs!

Our bodies are priceless and they deserve the best of everything that we can give them.

Ask yourself:

- Do you love your body?

- Do you respect her?

- Do you nourish Her?

- Do your treat her with love, compassion and care?

- Do you do the best for her?

- Do you trust her?

- Do you restrict her with rules?

- Do you punish her with too much activity?

- Do you ever take a moment and listen to her?

- Do you feel disgusted by her?

- Are you grateful for her and everything that she does for you?

- Do you abuse her verbally, or physically?

Remember, that in your one chance on this planet, your one go at life, you only get **ONE** body!

The more you abuse her, the shorter your life experience will be.
You need to nourish, love, respect and care for your body in order to enjoy the best of life's little adventures.

Remember, you are not at war with your body, you are at war with your own thoughts, expectations and beliefs.

In order to turn this war around to a peaceful resolution, you need to start caring for and nourishing your body, making her feel special and loved, treating her like a cherished friend, And in time, with patience, YOU will start to love her more than anyone else, and your mind will start to love you!

Then, and only then will the battles that you encounter with your own thoughts start to transform to peaceful, loving and nurturing conversations filled with happiness and joy!

A Sugar Coated Secret Love Affair

Have you ever had a relationship with someone that you never truly *"got over"*, you know, the one that got away?
If you have, then you will probably know that you can never truly love another until you learn to let go of the past!
You could be dating the most gorgeous person on the planet, but still be thinking of another.

Well, food and our relationship with it, can be very similar - it is like a sugar coated secret love affair!

You could eat all of the super salads, smoked salmon and power smoothies that you like, but if you are still hung up and kicking yourself over a piece of chocolate cheese cake that you ate two weeks ago, well, this isn't good!
This is not a healthy mindset and will not serve you, or your body moving forwards.

You need to learn to let go of the past, as you wont achieve a healthy body without a healthy mindset.

There was a time when I thought that food didn't really matter, as long as I was killing myself in the gym! But very soon after I invested some time and money into a rigorous nutrition coaching programme, I came to realise that food is way more than just *"fuel"* for my body.

Nutrition is the key to health, happiness, energy, strength, life and so much more,

It is so crucially important that we nurture our bodies with good, honest, healthy, wholesome and nourishing foods.

BUT, more importantly, without a healthy mindset, without love, care and respect for yourself and your body, without understanding why you eat what you eat and your relationship with food, your journey to happiness could be thwarted with fear, doubt, regret, anxiety, pain and yes, relapse.

One of my most important coaching points with my clients is never to set rules.
There will never be a conversation when I say:
"You can't eat this" *or* "you can only eat that".
This method does not work, these rules make a diet, and as we all know, diet's don't work.

Understanding your relationship with food is vital for long term changes.

Over the years of training and coaching women, I have learnt a great deal about nutrition and behaviour, and I suspect that I will always be learning more. But one of the biggest "penny drop" moments has been to realise that you can't TELL people what to do, you can set goals, or write meal plans.

The very essence of human nature is to question and doubt, especially when it comes to something as messed up and confusing as diets and nutrition.

In fact, when coaching my clients, I ask only one thing of them, one very simple action before they eat.

To THINK!!!

To THINK about how they feel.
To THINK whether or not they are hungry.
To THINK if the food serves them and their body well.
To THINK about tasting the food.
To THINK about savouring the food.
To THINK if the food is helping them to feel good.

I do not ask if the food was healthy, unhealthy, good bad or indifferent, in fact, I try not to label foods and put them into boxes.
Because boxes equal rules, rules equal diets and diets don't work!

Food is a sensory thing, to eat, to chew, to taste, to savour. It is an experience!

I ask my clients to look at food, and the action of eating as a much bigger picture. To look through the panoramic viewing window of life and go beyond boxes, categories, labels or nutritional value.

To THINK!

What is this food to me and my body?
What is this food doing for me and my body?
What is this food giving to me and my body?
Why am I eating this food?

Take your time, slow down, notice!

SLOW DOWN!

In order to taste and savour your foods, you need to slow down. You NEED to chew! You need to savour!

Chewing your food for longer has many benefits, not just that it gives your stomach time to prepare to digest, and helps to improve the process of digestion.
But also, regardless of the food that you are putting in, if you are not taking your time, thinking, chewing and tasting, then even the "healthiest" of foods can still cause you problems.

When I was eating a *"diet"* of just chicken and salad, or chicken and broccoli, I felt so deprived by my restrictions that I would literally pour food into my mouth. I barely chewed and simply swallowed the food whole.

Wow... is it possible to liquify chicken.... That may have been only marginally quicker!

I was so far away from listening to my body, that I barely noticed that I was even eating, or what I was eating!
What I did notice though, was how my stomach hurt after eating, and how constipated I was.
How my stomach and bowels were cramping constantly, and that I was in a state of perma-worry about when, and if I might need to go to the toilet!

Yeah, I only noticed the negative!

Food doesn't actually digest so well when you practically inhale it, and all I was achieving by eating like this was a heightened sense of the *"Fuck you body"* attitude!

But, it wasn't my body, it wasn't my body at all!
It was all of my restrictions, rules, routines and ridiculousness!

I guess you could say I was binge eating healthy foods!

But a binge is a binge, regardless of what goes in!

What I realised was the act of bingeing, the act of all of these rules and regulations, restrictions and routines was a distraction from what was really going on.

It was a decoy mechanism!

By focusing on food, blaming food, feeling bad about my eating behaviours and getting angry with my body (*fuck you body*), I was ignoring the real problem.

I was ignoring what was making me unhappy in the first place, and it wasn't my body shape.
I was missing something in my life, I had a void, a chasm of chaos inside my head that was diverting the negative flow of unhappiness to my body and to my food.

In short, I was dealing with, or maybe even creating one problem, to avoid dealing with another, more painful one.
Another problem that had plagued me for longer than I even really knew. (The loss of my dad!).

My dad was a legend, my hero, idol, protector, favourite all round person in the whole wide world!
I was daddies little girl, the blonde haired, blue eyed, can "do no wrong" apple of his eye.
The youngest of four siblings, and the most spoilt!

But when I was 17, my dad died in a car accident, and my whole world fell to pieces... and I mean literally shattered into a million pieces, and I don't think I ever really recovered from that until I was about 35!

I crashed out of just about everything that I tried, other than drinking until it didn't hurt any more. This later became drugs, and then later turned into anger management issues.

I got over the drugs pretty quickly, that only lasted about a year, and was never an addiction, just an escape from reality, an escape from the pain!

I came to realise that I had never grieved, I never said goodbye and I never got to kiss him good night ever again. And kissing him good night was a bit of a game... we would try and see who could give the most kisses each night... I would usually win by pinning him to the sofa until his big, prickly moustache would make my face itch.

Shit, I loved that man... and damn, I miss him!!!

But this was what was screwing me up now, in adulthood, many years later - in life and in happiness. I had never got over that one true love, and I couldn't love myself, let alone truly love anyone else. And neither could I let anyone else love me, not properly, not fully. I closed down the love factory so to speak!

And, I took it all out on my own body!
I simply changed the pain! Diverted the pain to somewhere else, something else that I could deal with.

I eventually sought help from a spiritual healer, to help me find peace with the loss of my dad and the advice that she gave to me was perfect... and it worked.

I finally got to say goodbye, to cry for my dad and to feel at peace with his departure. I felt like the world, and most of the universe had been lifted from my shoulders, I was born again, I felt lighter, free-er, happier!

With the acceptance and closure of this, I was able to turn my attention to myself. And almost immediately I was able to hear the faint cries of my own body.
Her drowned out whispers!
Some for joy that I was noticing her, that I had come home! And some of frustration that I had been away for so long.

Recognise the real issues, then combat the other shit!

I urge you as a women, as a dieter, as a self-hater and as a friend to sit with your problems, recognise them and deal with them however you need to.

Once you have jumped the first hurdle, you will be able to see the next. You will have time to prepare for it, and give yourself the energy and belief you need to clear it with ease.

Rather than attacking yourself, your body and your mind, rather than filling yourself with a negative, self-loathing commentary, nurture your relationship with your mind and body, and stop using food and your relationship with "diets" as an outlet of the internal hurts that you may be feeling.

Some of the *"hurts"* that my clients have come to realise include:

- Being bullied as a child at school

- An abusive partner or family member
- Harsh parenting
- Negative or derogatory teachers
- Emotional Abuse
- Work stresses or redundancy
- Family pressures
- Physical violence
- The loss of a loved one
- Relocating homes/families
- Lack of love or intimacy from family/partner

And many more, the list is endless and different for everyone.

Remember, we are all at war with something!

_____

I chose a more spiritual path to freedom, something that was completely different from conventional methods.
Seeking the universal energy, wisdom, strength, light and power.
I turned my attention to enlightenment, to deeper connection, to the universe.
This method has helped me in so many ways over the years, that I went one step further and trained to become a Reiki Master, to heal the chakras and seek answers through meditation.
And, although I know that this approach will not work for everyone, I honestly believe and trust that this route was my calling, my gift and my answer to all of my hurts.

We live in a world, and a society that causes huge rifts in our own personal connections. The connection we feel to ourselves, our bodies, thoughts, dreams and desires.

We have disconnected from our bodies, and from other people, and this needs to change.
We seem to love things more than we love people, and certainly more than we love ourselves.
In fact, we should love people and use things, and in many cases, we love things and use people!

This is a twisted way to live our lives, and wont help in achieving a healthy mindset or finding happiness.

We need to reconnect with our own selves, reconnect with our body and listen, hear, feel and be present with our own selves.
We need to nurture our relationships in order to grow them, allowing them to blossom into beautiful, strong, life long friendships that care for each other.
We need to open up our mind to our body, start listening, and hearing the raw truth of how we are treating her!
She is your BEST friend! Love her!

Start looking within yourself and seeking the answers that your body has been trying to give you since the day you were born.
Listen to your intuition, your gut feelings, your emotions.
Feel the pains, pay attention to her!!!

You may be a little shocked with what you learn about yourself!

But this is a journey of self exploration, self discovery and self improvement, so embrace those moments, embrace those feelings and discoveries and embrace those light bulb moments that allow your heart to open up to your body, mind, spirit and soul.

Listen Up!

The first moment of the rest of your life is the moment that you feel, not the moment that you think!

Listen Up and Pay Attention

When I was studying my Cognitive Behavioural Therapy and Mindfulness programmes, it became very clear to me that in order to truly improve our own relationship with our body, with our mind, with our self and with our food, we need to become skilled in the art of observation... taking notice!

We needed to switch on and tune in!
We needed to look in on ourselves from the outside!
We needed patience, kindness, love and compassion!
We needed to watch carefully, conscientiously and calmly!

We needed mindfulness!

In simple terms, mindfulness is just a way of thinking, it isn't a rule book or a guide book, it isn't the right or wrong answers! But what it does give you, is choice!

Your relationship with food and your body needs mindfulness!

Let's just think about your relationship with food, so far you have tried to diet, on and off, one week good, one week bad, day after day, week after week, month after month, you have endured the relentless onslaught of dieting rules and restrictions.

This relationship is riddled with imperfections, unrealistic rules, neglect, arguments, hurt, tears and abuse.

This relationship does not sound very healthy or happy, do you think?

So consider this, what if this was a relationship with another person, a friend, a colleague, a boss or even a partner?

How would this kind of controlling, abusive and negative relationship make you feel?
What would you do if you were in this relationship?

Would you sit down and take it, or would you fight back?
Would you try to break free or remain feeling like you are shackled with no options?

What would you do?
How would you feel?

Sometimes, however, you simply cannot see the forrest for all of the trees.
When you are in a situation or predicament, you may not even be aware of it, not until you open your eyes, pay attention, listen to your body and make a choice!

Whether you choose to stay in the relationship or liberate yourself, that is entirely YOUR choice.
But you do have that choice.

You ALWAYS have a CHOICE!

And practising mindfulness can open up many of these choices to you!

Mindfulness takes practise, time and patience, but by unlocking the power of observation, sitting up and paying attention, will lead you to your future happiness!

Mindfulness is one of the most fundamental keys to creating your future self.
A future self that can love their body, love their flaws, love themselves and feel at peace with their own mind, their own decisions, actions and their own thoughts.

To be mindful is to be conscious!
It is a choice!
It is YOUR choice!

There are no rules, no restrictions, no failure, no backlash - only options!

Being mindful doesn't mean that you suddenly start attending a morning meditation class every week or going to the local yoga studio for daily flow classes! If you want to do these things, then that is your choice!

Being mindful simply means to be aware of your own thoughts and decisions.
To be consciously aware of what you are doing, why you are doing it and how your actions serve you and your future self!

As I said in the last chapter, all I ask my clients to do is TO THINK!

For example, I remember regularly visiting a local coffee shop with a friend and always ordering the same thing, a cappuccino, frothy coffee at it's finest. I never even thought about it, I just ordered it!
I never considered the options, even if I was stood in the queue waiting for a while.
That order would just roll off of the tongue like silk.

Being mindful in this situation, would have meant walking into that same coffee shop and **THINKING** about what I was going to order, rather than just allowing my usual order to fall right off of my mouth.

To consider the options!
To choose consciously!
To be aware and to be present!

The simply action of ordering a coffee has been hijacked by your own subconscious brain, it has become a habitual behaviour.
It requires no thought!
But how many other regular actions have been hijacked?
Which choices are yours and which are your subconscious?
Who decided what you should wear this morning?
Who thought about your route to work?
Who fastened your skirt zipper?

By allowing the subconscious to hijack our thoughts and actions, we are giving up our own freedom of choice, we are kind of being held prisoner by our own minds!

Hey, subconscious brain, SHUT UP! Fuck you brain!!!

Think about it, how many times have you driven to work or the shops, and almost immediately after arriving, not been able to remember driving?

Yes, we've all done it!

Things that we do most regularly, like driving, eating, drinking, dressing, washing, even toilet breaks are so habitual, that we simply do not need to think about them anymore.

We just flick on the "auto-pilot" switch and away we go! We basically vacate the premises and let our subconscious mind deal with our body.

We are a prisoner of our subconscious brain!
It is holding all of the control until we demand it back and become awake & mindful!
Until we start listening and noticing!

Hey, this is my body! I am taking her back!

When practising mindfulness, I always recommend that you begin by just listening to your thoughts.
Taking notice of how you are feeling, and not judging your thoughts. Do not feel anger or resentment towards them, your mind is just doing what it has always done.
It is you that is making the change now!

Question your thoughts, and allow this inquisitive side of you to guide your actions.

In doing so you will begin reconnecting with your body, listening to the cues and clues that she is offering you.

Follow the breadcrumb trail and find out what your body really wants.

I found this method of questioning really useful when I was trying to simply hydrate my body more effectively.

You see, I drink a lot of water, but I am terrible with my consistency on a day to day basis.

My weakness was diet soda!

I would grab a can of the fizzy stuff instead of water, it was habitual.

However, when I started to question what the fizzy drink was doing for me and my body, it helped me choose the water.
The more water I drank to replace the soda, the better my body started to feel.
The better my body started to feel the less I wanted to drink the soda.

Eventually, I found that I didn't even want soda any more, and that I would automatically pour a glass of water.

I have barely had even a sip of any soda since. And, I stress that this is not a rule that I have set myself, it is by choice. I know that I can still choose to have a fizzy drink at any time, I just don't want one.
I am free to choose!

My body feels awesome as a result, my action of drinking water has become habitual and I have never set a single rule or restriction to achieve this.
I just paid attention to how I felt!
How my body felt!
I listened!

This method of mindfulness, awareness, questioning works for any other kind of food or drink, as long as you stay connected to and listen to your body.
Trust her, she knows what is good for you!

Questions are always a fantastic tool, so here are a few that you may want to consider asking yourself and your body:

- What can I do today to support and love my body?
- What is my body telling me right now?
- What will help me and my body to feel good together?
- Am I seeing any patterns in my thoughts/feelings/actions?

Remember, listen to your thoughts, listen to your body, but don't judge what you hear.
Just listen, observe and take notice.
Be curious!
Investigate!
Learn!

In order to heal and repair, you need to be a student of your own body.
Be a good student and listen carefully!

Food is information for the body!
Give your body all of the best information in order to receive the best outcome.

The Exciting New Relationship

Hold on, let's slow down for just a moment.
Take a moment for air and to think....

Have you established what is causing you pain?
What area of your life is causing the emotional
diversion and leading to the relationship that you are
having with your food and your body?

Have you found the real pain?

If you haven't found this pain yet, then take some time
to think, feel, listen and understand what you are doing,
what you are thinking.
What is hurting you?

Finding the root cause of your pain can surface some
really old feelings and memories from the past. But if
they stay rooted within you, they will continue to cause
you more pain. It's a bit like a weed in your flower bed,
you need to "get it" at the root to prevent it from
regrowing.

Find a metaphorical shovel and start digging around,
move the dead leaves and debris about and see what
you can uncover.

I remember when I first visited my reiki master for my
initial treatment, I already had an idea of what was
causing my pain, I chose not to tell her anything, but
she felt it too.

Her advice to me, which has been one of the most
valuable pieces of advice in my life, was to spend some
time alone, meditate and think only about my father.

Not to be all mystic and call upon him or try to speak with him, but just carry all of the thoughts of my dad into my meditation.
To lose myself in those thought!

As skeptical as I was, I did this.

I took the Rose Quartz crystal she had gifted to me in one hand, a photo of my dad in the other hand, and with some soothing music in the background, I just lay back on my bed, eyes closed and thought about my dad.

About the kisses good night, the encouragement, the tellings off I would get when I was naughty, the trips away with him for work, the playing at the stables at the weekends.

Call me crazy, but after a while, I felt as though my dad was with me.
I felt as though I could speak to him, hug him, kiss him goodnight one more time and tell him I love him.
I could finally, after nearly 16 years, say my good byes.

At which point, I jolted upright on my bed with tears flooding down my cheeks, I cried and cried and cried. I don't remember ever crying so hard in my life.
But I wasn't sad.
I wasn't hurting!
I felt free!
I felt lighter!
I felt at peace!

I am not telling you to meditate, unless you want to… remember, you always have the choice… But what I am suggesting to you is that you simply sit alone with your problem, your pain, your issue and you just think about it.
Think about what it makes you feel, what it does for your life, your body, your soul, your happiness.
What it does for YOU!
Just sit with it and ask questions.
Explore, investigate and learn!

This method may not work for you the first time you try it, maybe not even the second time, but if you continue to face your pain, the answers will come.
And they will give you the clarity that you need to understand what you need to do, and how you need to repair before you tackle the relationship that you have with your body, your food and your thoughts.

_____

Earlier, I gave you the example of an abusive relationship, and asked what if you were in this situation?
Let's be honest, we would all like to think that we would be able to remove ourselves from this kind of scenario.

However, we cannot take ourselves away from the relationship that we have with food.
We need food! Without it, well, we would starve, and that would not be so good.

We can't just walk away, instead we need to repair this relationship, we need to find a way to love food in a way that allows food to love us back.

We need food to be fun, exciting, and adventurous.

We need food to light up our senses and make our bodies sing with delight.

We need our relationship to be like the honeymoon period of any relationship - fresh, exhilarating, new and sensory.

By establish and spending time with our original pain, the pain that is diverting to emotional eating and self-berating, the possibilities become endless.

The healing work that you achieve through acceptance, forgiveness or just simply understanding the pain, can lift the fog that surrounds your own beliefs and behaviours.

No longer will you be pulled backwards by internal hurts, but liberated free to explore yourself and your body.

Sometimes, this is all it takes for some of my clients to start hearing their bodies, to start caring more, listening more closely and treating their body with the love and respect that she deserves.

And sometimes, it takes a little more time.

But, if you can start connecting with your body, start listening, hearing and feeling, you will be able to start flowing postive energy and love in.

To think is to feel!
To feel is to see!
To see is to believe!

Up & Down Up & Down Up & Down

I have lost count of the amount of times that I have spoken to a new client and they have irrefutably denied "yo-yo" culture.

But whilst listening to their story, their past attempts, their thoughts, emotions, reasoning and so on, all I can see in my mind is a yo-yo going up and down, up and down, up and down.

Denial is a tough cookie to crack. You see, the problem with denial, is even when you know that you are suffering it, you still deny it! It's the very nature of the beast.

Have you ever said any of the following phrases or followed these behaviours:

- I will start on Monday.
- I will start AGAIN on Monday.
- Latest celeb diet in latest magazine said I should….
- Asking others what diet they are on.
- Asking others how many calories they are eating.
- Asking other people what they weigh, and then-
- Comparing your body to theirs.
- Labelling foods "good" or "bad"
- Labelling days as "good" or 'bad"
- Labelling weeks as "good" or "bad"
- Saving calories for the weekend so that you can binge.
- Swapping from one diet to another, or removing one food group or another.
- I have fallen off the wagon.
- Tracking EVERYTHING that you eat.

- Constantly thinking about the next meal.

Yeah, I know, how do I know all of this....?

Because I have been there my friends. It is sad but true, even with the latest and greatest fitness qualifications, we're just as confused and screwed up as every body else (*hence why I went back to school to learn about REAL nutrition*).

When I was battling with my own demons, I would crash the wagon not just off of the track, but off of the side of a cliff....
That wagon was not going to be able to get back on track, it was in pieces. I would need to rebuild it from scratch!

I would constantly label things, look at what was in other peoples shopping trolleys, look at the latest magazines, feel jealous of someone half my age who had flat abs... oh to be 19 again.
I would always be saying next Monday, next Monday, NEXT Monday.
Stripping carbs, removing saturated fats, upping protein, removing bread, taking the latest supplement, believing the hype and falling hook, line and sinker for the promises of a better body and so on.

I don't know about you, but I found it exhausting! I literally felt like I could have slept for a month sometimes, and perhaps would've if given the chance.

I thought this next one would be THE one, this time would be THE time, this diet would be THE diet, this routine would fix all of my problems.
I'd finally be happy!

But none of them did... Meal plan after meal plan failed me, but at that moment in time, I thought I had failed them!
Fuck you body!!!!

Eat ~Sleep ~ Weigh ~ Repeat!!!

How many of these scenarios have you been in, which phrases have you said or behaviours have you shown?

Well, news flash, if you have found yourself doing any of these, regularly, on and off, or all of the time, then you, I am afraid to tell you, are trapped in the Yo-Yo Culture.

It is time to let the string snap and jump off!
Let the yo-yo roll away!
It'll be fun, I promise!

If you change the way you look at things, the things you look at will change!

Friend, Foe or Frenemy?

Have you ever felt like food is calling you?
Calling your name in a sultry and irresistible manner from the fridge?
Goading you to come and indulge, enjoy, binge?

It may sound a little crazy, I know, food cant actually talk, right?

But do you ever feel as though your every thought is centred around food?
Meals, choices, calories, what's next, what's next, what's next?

Or do you ever feel as though you have lost control? No matter how much you resist food, try to stay on track, try to eat the right things, make the right choices, you eventually realise that food is in fact actually controlling you?

These thoughts plague the minds of most of us!

You are not crazy or obsessed with food, no!
But you may be a little obsessed with the dieting lifestyle, the yo-yo culture and of course, losing weight, changing your body, finding your happiness.

But, in reality, another new diet isn't going to change any of this!
The next diet wont repair your mindset, your relationship with yourself, your mind, your body or with food itself.

In fact, it is the diet industry that has created this sense of obsession, this way of life for you, and I am sad to say, that this is the exact outcome that they wanted to achieve.

I have heard many of my clients say that they are addicted to food or addicted to sugar. That they can't live without chocolate or bread or crisps or biscuits. Some have even joked about booking in for rehab. (*I say that they joked, but I really got the sense that if they could, if it were possible, they would actually book into rehab*).

Although none of these "*can't live without*" foods are really an addiction, we do as humans, use them in the same manner as some more potent and addictive substances like alcohol, sex, drugs etc.

Remember how I said earlier in the book that I used alcohol and drugs so I couldn't feel any more, to numb the pain?
It's a coping mechanism, a comforter, a way to escape the real pain that you are carrying around with you.

But a drug or alcohol abuser can remove the problem, they can book into rehab or go cold turkey to remedy the addiction.
But we cannot do this with food!
We need food to survive, it is essential to our health and vitality.

We can't set these hard hitting rules around our food choices and behaviours, this becomes a diet, and we all know and understand that diets don't work!

But, when you bring all of these points together, it all just deepens the problem and makes our already fractious relationship with food, even worse!

We need to find a way to love food so that food can love us in return. Feed our body, minds, spirit and soul with joy.

You need to establish your true pain, sit with it, work with it and settle it.

You need to break free and liberate yourself from the diet lifestyle and yo-yo culture.

You need to work on your mindset and live free of rules, restrictions, routines and guilt when it comes to your food.

You need to take charge of your obsessive eating patterns and start to pay attention to your body.

You need to recognise and practise how to be mindful about your choices and your eating.

You need to start believing in yourself, your body, your mind and begin to enjoy life from within a beautiful headspace that allows you to live without fear, doubt, shame or judgement.

You need to start living life and loving it from the body and mind of a healthy and happy women.

You need to let go!

_____

I asked a handful of my own friends and followers to describe their relationship with food in just five words, and these are just some of the responses that I received:

- An out of control mess.
- Food is my biggest frenemy.
- I can't live without food.
- Food and I don't mix.
- I love, yet hate food.
- Food is my saviour & controller.
- Food calls my name… Heeeellleeeen!
- I eat because I'm unhappy.
- I can't stick to diets.
- I'd do anything for bread.
- I count, track, fail, binge!
- I live in a vicious cycle.
- I feel permabad about food.
- I don't really understand food.
- Love, hate, want, binge, guilt!
- I can't stop myself sometimes.
- Regret! I feel let down!

And these weren't even all of the responses, some people couldn't keep within the five words, and some managed to summarise it in one word.
Some of those included:

- Non-Existent
- Terrible
- The Worst
- Painful
- Regret
- Disgust
- Resentful
- Appalling
- Shocking

- Failing
- Frenemy
- Gross
- Lazy
- Uninspired

Just spend a second and read all of those again - how many of them sound like a fun and fulfilling way to live?

Do any of them sound like the kind of relationship that you want to be a part of - for the rest of your life?

How much of your life have you already wasted feeling this way about food and yourself?
How much more are you going to waste?

The word "frenemy" came up quite a few times in the responses, "Food is my frenemy!"

Which brings me to another point.

When I first started working with women as a personal trainer, over a decade ago, I had an email series that I would send to new clients, one particular episode was titled
"Fat is Friend, Not Foe!"

But the problem goes way deeper than people believing fat is bad. It goes way deeper than any of the macronutrients, fats, carbs or proteins.

As time passed, that email series, and the title became
"FOOD is friend, not foe!"

Food is an amazing thing, and maybe we all just take it for granted, maybe we see it in the wrong way, with the wrong perspective.

When I studied nutrition and nutrition coaching, the first page of my course text book set out a whole new perspective for me.

In that first page, I learned the biggest and most valuable lesson of the entire course.

I learned something that changed my entire outlook of food and eating.

Food is way more than just fuel for our body!

Food is like our connection to mother nature, our source of light, power, energy, life, joy and so much more.

Food is like Gaia giving you a massive hug to let you know that everything will be ok. To soothe you and nurture you.

Food is life, love, comfort, reassurance and hope!

The topic of food goes much deeper than just this, but for this moment, let's just stay here and talk about how food can be perceived as the frenemy.

Think of all of the times that food has been there for you!

After a stressful day at work, she reached out and calmed you down.

After a fight with a loved one, she pulled you in and told you that everything would be ok.

After all of life's big and little ups and downs, food has always been there and she has always known how to just make shit feel better!

She gives you pleasure, comfort, release, happiness. She picks you up when you are down and gives you life when you feel tired.

But, she also knows how to bowl you over.
She knows how to keep it real, and serve up a pinch of reality.
She knows how to make you want more, crave more, eat more!

And, sooner or later, this beautiful relationship starts to breakdown as you realise what is actually happening. This relationship is suddenly met with resentment, anger, despair and confusion!

"FOOD - how could you do this to me? I thought you loved me? Why would you hurt me?"

And this is when the lightbulbs illuminate. The idea of diets start to form in your head.
All of the hurt, the cover ups, the *"you're not good enough!"*, the *"you need to change"*, the *"you're piling it on, fatty"* all lead to one catastrophic conclusion.
We NEED to diet! We NEED Control!

So, maybe food is the frenemy?
Maybe there is a darker side to her?
Or maybe, she is manufactured this way?

And that is the key word in this whole chapter.... MANUFACTURED!

Just like the diet industry wants you to fail, the food industry wants you to want more.
It's like a conspiracy!

Maybe it is a conspiracy?
There's something to think about!

But this was where my opinion, my attitude and my beliefs all changed, because much like you, I too thought that food was the frenemy!

But, that first day of nutrition school, on that first page of my massive text book, there was a short sentence that changed it all!
"REAL food is way more than just fuel!"

"Yeah… Don't I know it! She's a complete bitch"

NO! Hold up! That was the old me, the victim!
I am not a victim!
I am a strong and confident woman! A beautiful and independent women in control of my own life and my own destiny.
Are you a victim?

So, what is real food?

Real food = LOVE!

On that first day of nutrition school, I learnt that REAL food is love! And when you fill your body with love, you get love back!
The more you give, the more you get and the more you feel loved in return.
Love for your body is born, or more accurately, reinstated!

Real food is information!
Real food gives your body all of the information that it needs.
It gives the body nutrients to feed, fuel, heal and nurture!
It gives the body a big hug of goodness, rather than just giving you a hug of comfort.

Food, with all of its glorious colours and combinations, is our story, our legacy, our culture, our religion.
It tells a tale of our upbringing, our heritage, our family.
It speaks about where we come from and our family values, the love we received as a child.

Food is life and love!

Food is way more than a comfort blanket or fuel!

Food is EVERYTHING!

Real transformation requires real honesty. If you want to move forward - Get real with yourself!

Bryant McGill

The True Transformation

It kinda hurts me to say this, but for many of the years that I was a personal trainer, I indulged, and fell for the lie that is: **Slim = Happy!**

You may have seen those transformation photos on social media and thought,
"Wow, way to go lady!"

But just because they have achieved this huge physical change, doesn't mean that they have achieve the ultimate goal of happiness.
I think, last time I checked it was upwards of 94% of women who achieve their weight loss goal WILL regain the weight eventually.
That's shocking, right?

These amazing and inspirational women who have transformed their lifestyles and their bodies will still face the same burdens as you or I.
I know this, because I have seen many of my earlier clients (*pre-mindset coaching days*) relapse as soon as we have parted ways.

The root cause of the problem hadn't been addressed, no sorry, let me rephrase that, it hadn't even been acknowledged, let alone addressed.

So the moment that they experienced pain or fear or hurt, the old binge behaviour would rise up, bubbling under the skin ready to boil over.
The true pain was still burning a hole in their soul, until one day, the pain became so great that the bubble would burst, and binge they would!

It's a bit like the first pee of the night out, you know that once that "seal" is broken, that's it!
You are up and down to the loo every 20 or 30 minutes, and this only worsens as we get older ladies!
And so does the bubbling pains and binge behaviour!

To achieve a true transformation, one that brings you love, happiness and peace, the changes don't necessarily need to happen to your body, at least not at first. They need to happen in your mind!

The real transformation happens when you begin to feel, to care, to love, to appreciate, to enjoy!

The love and care that you feel towards yourself transcends into your behaviours, into your actions, into your choices and into your lifestyle, you begin to love your body!
And in return, your body begins to love you back!

When you achieve this kind of transformation, when your body starts to love you back, your body will begin to change, rewarding you for the love, the care, the appreciation.

When you transform your mind, you transform from the inside out.
You will not only see changes in your body, but in your life too.

But how can you capture these kind of awesome changes in a before and after photograph?
How can you show others what you have achieved?

You can't really! Not in that way!

Only you and your closest friends and family can see through your smile and see what is lying deeper underneath.

Fake smile Vs Real smile!

But, this kind of transformation doesn't need to be captured in a moment, in a staged photograph.
No! It is captured in every action you make!

How you act, how you behave, how you talk, what you talk about, who you spend your time with, how you enjoy your time, what you share in your life, how you dress, how you are more confident than ever before, how you laugh, joke, smile, how you eat and what you eat.

EVERY ACTION SHOWS YOUR TRANSFORMATION! AND EVERY ACTION LOCKS IN YOUR TRANSFORMATION!

I remember when I first started to notice my own transformation, people would comment:
"Are you ok? I noticed you are acting differently?"
"How are you? I saw your post on social media, you seemed different!"

And ladies, this is crucial, do not be afraid of *"different"*.
Different is good!
Different means change!
"Different" means people are noticing something about you, but they do not know, or understand what!

Change is Good!
Different is GOOD!

Change is psychological, not physical!

So next time you see one of those transformation photographs on the internet, give the respect due to this beautiful human being who has achieved something quite extraordinary. But remember, if they haven't acknowledged, addressed and healed their root pain, their true hurts, then they could relapse at any moment.

And, that is a really sad thing, because is not easy to make that kind of physical change!

Respect their efforts!
Respect their dedication and hope that they have healed inside enough to maintain their amazing achievement!

———————————

Another note to mention here is, don't think that this person has found a secret that you haven't!

They have just abided by the rules for a really long time, probably with numerous ups and downs along the way.
Those rules and restrictions will still very much be in play, and are still just as likely to come crashing down.
REVOLT!

Will Power!

Just because this complete stranger that you have seen pictured in a before and after photo has stuck to the rules, doesn't mean that they have a gargantuan supply of will power either.

I like to think of will power as an *"anti-intuition"* mechanism.

A serious disconnect from both emotions, intuition and of course the body! A ticking time bomb!
Whether we are aware of it or not, this disconnect is the likely cause of self sabotage and further self loathing.

In fact, the less will power you demonstrate, the better. To me, this just means that you are more in tune and connected to the things that really matter - your body, your mind, your spirit, your soul and your self!
Intuition is telling you *"fuck all these rules, they don't work, I don't like them!"*

LISTEN TO HER!
IT'S NATURAL!

You are naturally listening to your body when you *"go off track!"*.

Will Power = Disconnection!

Intuition is the Whispers of the Soul

Our Own "Ism's"

We are all individual and unique, and all have *"ism's"* that are personal and our own.
None of these *"ism's"* can really be changed, as they are you. They are in essence, what make you, you!

In fact, as part of my initial interview process with new clients, I work through a questionnaire that is called the "You-Nique" experience.
(I think we should change the spelling from Unique to YOUnique! It totally fits and works, don't you agree?)

But as humans, we all have tendencies, and these tendencies can determine how we act, think, behave and live up to expectations.

If you have heard of Gretchen Rubin then you may be familiar with her work within this field. If you have never heard of her, then I highly recommend that you go and seek out her books once you have finished this one.

The theory is that we all have a tendency, whether we are an upholder - who follows the rules and meets all expectations. An obliger who meets the expectations of others, but not of themselves. A questioner who needs to know all of the facts when meeting expectations of others, but easily meets their own expectations. OR, like me, a rebel who basically fights against all expectations, even their own.

If you know which of the tendencies that you most resemble, then you can start to make small and subtle changes to your language, so that you are able to meet more of those expectations, regardless of where or who they come from.

Our "ism's" have a great deal to do with why diets wont work as well. You see all of the rules and restrictions that make up a diet or tailored meal plan or even a meal plan that you have plucked out of a shiny celeb-worshipping magazine is, that they do not take into consideration your "ism's", your priorities, your strengths, weaknesses, likes, dislikes....

They do not consider anything to do with you, or your LIFE!

- A busy work schedule or business trip
- A sick child, relative or even yourself
- Your cravings
- Your level of activity
- Your sleep and wake cycles
- Your menstrual cycle
- Your hormone balance or imbalance
- Your relationships
- Your social life (*if you have one*)
- Your location in the world and it's climate or available foods
- Your hydration, electrolytes and salt levels.
- Your general health
- Your mental health
- Your body type, frame, size or shape
- Your blood type
- Your intolerances or allergies
- Your culture, religion, genetics
- YOUR INDIVIDUAL NEEDS

There are so many things that are missing, overlooked, ignored, and this is deliberate, because as I mentioned earlier, diets are created to fail you!

They are designed and created to make you feel worse, make you come back again and again for another attempt! Spend more and more of your hard earned cash on bogus products to help you succeed.
They make you feel as though you are a failure!
AND YOU ARE NOT!

Your will power, your desire to change, your *"ism's"* all have absolutely zero to do with diets not working for you!

You can only achieve the changes that you want, once you take theme to sit back and listen.
Take notice of your body!
Hear what she is saying to you!
Listen to your thoughts, take notice of what you are saying to yourself.
LISTEN!

Only when you start to feel and hear, will you be able to transform!

I know that I keep saying you need to sit up and pay attention, hear your body and listen, and I get it, you are probably screaming at the pages of this book "HOW? How do I hear it? How do I listen?"

Everything will start to click in to place, you will be able to hear, feel, listen and observe, it just takes a little time.

And before then, you need to surrender to your body, trust in her and leave all of the rules and restrictions of diets behind you.

It's not just about listening, hearing and feeling your body, you also need to be able to recognise what she is telling you.

You need to understand the difference between emotional eating, habitual eating, cravings and real hunger.

You need to be able to feel your way around different emotions, and believe whole-heartedly in what your body is telling you.

You need to have faith and trust!

You need to recognise when your body has had enough and when you are full.

When to stop!

And in order to do this, you need to wave that little white flag to your body and say, *"Right, we're in this together, let's work through it together. Talk to me. Tell me what you need, what you want!"*.

You need a mindset that allows you to naturally and instinctively understand both your body and your food, so that the two become intrinsically bonded together.

You hear your body, you know what she wants and you are able to provide for and nurture her, so that she is able to feel the best she has ever felt.

It's a sad truth that most people have absolutely no idea what *"feeling good"* actually feels like.

They have never felt their best, and they have never known how to feel their best, or how to feed their body to feel her best.

It all comes down to not seeing the bigger picture, not listening to the cues or recognising the cries.

When your mindset evolves into one of self love, you stop being drawn in by momentary cravings, you stop hearing the signals that old habits are sending to you. You stop falling for the trashy foods and start falling in love with the nurturing ones.

Sometimes you might fancy a nice refreshing, colourful salad, with nuts and seeds and lots of wholesome deliciousness, and sometimes you might want some chocolate.
And that's totally cool!

But listening, hearing and understanding the body and her wants, that is the key to setting yourself free from dietary devastation and rules to revolt against.

You need to honour your body!
Give her the trust that she deserves.
She is an evolutionary masterpiece, and has more wisdom and knowledge than you allow her credit for.

TRUST HER!

There is a deep connection that runs between your mind, your body and your food, and to master it is to be free.

Once you have mastered it, you will have an amazing relationship with food, with yourself, with life and with all of those amazing people within your life, for life!

Once you have mastered it, you will feel freedom and smugly turn the other cheek when diets attempt to lure you into their smutty, dirty little ways.

Right now, right at this moment, you may feel as though your body wants junk, you may feel as though you are addicted to sugar, or a certain food that always seems to beat you into submission, you may feel that this path is too treacherous and challenging.

But, I can assure you, habits that have formed over your entire life, spanning from childhood into adulthood, habits that are so deeply set in your mind are controlling your thoughts right now.

Not sugar or biscuits or cake or ice cream or crisps or burgers or anything else.

Your beliefs, your actions and your behaviours are a direct result of the habits that have formed throughout your lifetime. The habits created by various influences that you have been subjected to.

Your body at her finest, at her healthiest, at her most glorious does not crave junk, or sugar, or non-descript chemical additives, or flavourings, or colourants, or preservatives.
NO!

She craves a bounty of vitamins, minerals, nutrients and all of the goodness that is naturally available from the earth and all of its splendificant offerings.

She craves a caring, loving and rich lifestyle that feeds and nurtures her and the soul.

She craves all of the things that make her feel the best she can in order to give you the best, most wholesome and fulfilling life.

She craves REAL food!

Abundance is not something we acquire, it is something we tune into.

Wayne Dyer

You Are Not to Blame

It is sad for me as a coach, when I hear women saying that they are *"broken"*, *"to blame"* or *"at fault"*, because all of these thoughts and emotions simply fuel the belief that there is something wrong with us, something wrong with our bodies that we simply cannot fix... ergo - "I can never be happy!"

Have you ever said or thought:
* I would settle for ….
* I will never achieve ….
* I could never do that ….
* I am not worthy/good enough for ….
* I would love to be…. But …..

You see, these points are all basically a self-shaming justification that we are not good enough!
They fuel the very issues that needs fixing.

I disagree entirely with this down trodden belief that we can NEVER be happy.
Why can't we be happy?

We all deserve to feel good, feel happy, feel content, feel satisfied, feel worthy, feel loved!

So where does this down trodden attitude come from?

We were not born thinking like this, in fact when many of us were children we had dreams, we had expectations, we had aspirations.
But slowly as we ascend into adulthood these dreams, expectations and aspirations all start to burn out, dissipate into nothing. They start to fade into the ever growing stresses and unhappiness that is life.

We let *"life"* chew up our dreams and spit them back out with a hint of a condescending laugh, as if to say *"keep dreaming love!"*

What did you want to be when you were a little girl?

What set your heart, soul and mind on fire when you were a child?

Maybe you dreamt of being a glamorous singer, dancer or actress.
Maybe you wanted to work as a veterinarian, police officer or flight attendant.
Perhaps, you wanted to be a mother!

Me, I wanted to be an international show jumper! I wanted to be the youngest person to jump the Hickstead Derby, and conquer the derby bank!
I almost made it too!

For many of us, the reason that we end up in this whirlwind of self-loathing, self-berating and self-pity is the simple realisation that our reality does not match our expectations.
We haven't achieved what we wanted most!

We haven't achieved our biggest dreams, so therefore we must be a failure!

Not at all! You are not to blame!

In most cases, in most lives there is a pattern, a series of events that determines the outcome.
For me, I was so close to becoming what I had dreamed of my entire life, and at that moment, in that short time within my life, that was when my dad passed away.

My coping mechanism for that loss, was to rebel! To throw everything away. To destroy my own dreams, because, to me, without my dad there, it all felt worthless. I felt worthless!

I didn't fail at my dreams, I threw them away!

I mentioned earlier in the book how we are all at war with something, we all have our own root pains that cause us to divert the pain to somewhere more managable.

This was my root pain, the loss of my dad, but also my own reaction to rebel.
I felt lost!

In 2013, when I finally got back on a horse, when I brought myself a new horse and I started riding again, suddenly those dreams reignited, but the manifested in slightly different ways.
I felt happy, I felt at peace and I felt as though I was whole.

I started to compete again, not to the same level or in the same discipline, but my hunger, my dream, my ambition had been satiated and I was able to see through the fog that had stopped me from moving forwards.

This was also when I started to realise that I had never said good bye to my dad.
This was my turning point! Everything started to click for me.

You see, you are not broken, you are just not living the life that you had expected to be living. Your dreams and expectations were greater than what your reality is today.

And that's not a bad thing, it isn't that you have failed or your are not capable.
It is just that a series of events in your life changed your course and sent you towards another calling.
The universe has plans for all of us, and sometimes we just need to open our eyes to see them.

Much like I said earlier on, by spending time with your thoughts, sitting with your hurts and recognising them, you are able to start making sense of them.
Understand them.
Appease them!
And sometimes you can even reignite the passion of your childhood dreams.

Have you ever seen the talent shows on TV, women (and men) in their mid-life, with their back stories about how their dreams were put on hold for children, family, life, career?
It's the same principle.

So, think back... what did you want to be when you were a little girl?

Sit with it, meditate with it if you feel it will help.
Think about all of the amazing things you have achieved in life, despite not achieving this.
And is this even something that you still want now?
If you wanted to be a dancer, could you go to dance lessons?
If you wanted to sing, could you join a choir?

If you wanted to be a fashion designer, could you start making your own outfits?

Nothing is stopping you from recreating that dream in adulthood.
Go on out there and do it!

And remember, you are not to blame!
You are not broken!

Before I finish this chapter, there is more to this than just what you wanted to be when you were little.

The beliefs and thoughts that you hold about your ability to do, be or achieve things in your life are also the product of the influences that you have been subjected to throughout your life.

Maybe you had a teacher at school who would always "put you down", or a parent who was not very supportive. Perhaps you were bullied, or picked on as a child by other students at school or even your siblings.

Regardless of whether you endured, one, two or all of these scenarios, remember, that you are not broken.
Your thoughts are just a product of past events, experiences and beliefs.

As you start to listen to your body, your thoughts and your mind, as you start to repair the relationship that you have with food and explore a new healthier mindset and way of thinking, these situations will begin to change, these beliefs will change and you will start to change with them.

Just sit up and pay attention!

We only fall off the wagon when our own inner core needs and desires are not being met.

Kate Reardon

What If There Was No Wagon?

Here's a thought, what if there was no wagon?
What if there was no track?
What is there was nothing to fall off of?
No pedestal, no expectation, no rules, no boxes!

What if life was just life and you could live it freely and happily, without always having to think about the next thing?

How much time would you have to enjoy if there was no tracking? No counting? No planning? No rule book?

Now, there is a thought!

How much time would you have to ENJOY if there was no wagon or track?

We are all guilty of labelling things, putting things into pigeon holes and boxing them up into this, that or the other.
But in order to move forward happily, freely and without restriction, you need to stop boxing your foods, meals, days and weeks in to categories, good days, bad days, ok days, healthy foods, bad foods, and so on.

Stop being so critical and so judgemental!
It is not a healthy mindset to employ.

The same applies to the track and the wagon!

I said earlier that I crashed my wagon, I didn't just fall off the track I crashed off the cliff. My wagon was destroyed, and to be honest, I am glad that I never rebuilt it after that.

It only served to hold me back and restrict me even more.

Just leave the wagon in the shed and move forwards on foot, one step at a time, one day at a time!
There is no rush to get to your destination, take your time and slow down!

Every day we are faced with multiple decision, what to wear, what route to take to work, what to pack for the kids lunches, where to walk the dog, which shoes look best with this dress and what should I eat for tea!

Every day, a non stop barrage of questions and decisions.

Did you know that the average human mind has between 12,000 and 75,000 individual thoughts each day!
O.M.G. No wonder we feel so exhausted!

In amongst these thoughts are numerous illusions, false beliefs and poor eating habits that have built up over time, years in fact.
They create an unnecessary pressure to be a certain way, act a certain way, dress a certain way, feel a certain way, eat a certain way.

You are always trying to stay within the expectations that you and others have impressed upon you, you are trying to stay between the lines so to speak.

So, how do we stop judging our own actions?
How do we re-write the habits, the thoughts and the expectations?

Well, quite simply we just start!

We just start today, now, in this moment.
We hear a thought and we ask ourselves, is this thought serving me?
Is this thought helping me to nurture myself, my mind or my body?

We take ownership of our thoughts, our actions and our choices.
We own them for what they are!
They were not good, bad or indifferent, they were just YOU!

Let's say that at lunch time, Sandra brings in some chocolate muffins.
You decided to have one, and it tasted good.
Then you went back to your desk.
You thought no more of it.
There was no guilt! No pain! No Fear! No Judgement! No anger! No Resentment! No Blame! No nothing!

You just simply decided to eat a muffin, accepted it and carried on.

It's OK to enjoy food, it's OK to indulge! It's OK!

Yeah, so maybe that food isn't going to help you strive towards how you want to feel, maybe your body didn't love it!
But that's ok! Because you owned it!
That one moment does not make the whole of the day "*bad*", in fact, it doesn't even make that moment bad.

These things happen, as long as you own it and you accept it, accept that nothing bad happened, then you can move on!
You are human! Get on with the day! Learn from how your body reacted to the food, and move on!

Just make your next choice based on how you want to feel, and how you want your body to fee. Listen to your body, what does she want?

I didn't fall off the track. I crashed the wagon off a cliff... and that is where I left it!

Where is Home?

Earlier in the book I asked you what your body was worth to you?
Whether is was worth more than your house?
Your car?
Your designer handbags and sparkly jewellery?

Have you thought any more about this?

Now that you have read a little more of this book, has your opinion changed at all?

Is your body worth more to you now that it was then?

What has changed?

In 2016 I held a free workshop speaking all about mindset, and if it was possible to change the habits that we have formed over a lifetime.
The first question that I asked in this workshop was:

Where is Home?

The looks on the audiences faces was one of confusion to start with, bemusement... What the heck does this have to do with weight loss, habits and mindset?

I pressed for an answer, and some said their street name, house number, estate, town and some even said the towns that they were born in.

And yes, technically they were all correct, but this wasn't quite the answer that I wanted from them.

I started to ask them the same few questions I have asked you.
What is your body worth, and so on.

How much would you enjoy life if your body let you down?

What would you be without your body?

I then asked the question again, "Where is home?"

One chirpy lady shouted out... "MY BODY!"

Wahey! Yes! Yes! Yes!

Your body is your one true home, the only home that you will ever have and the only accessory that you will carry with you from the moment that you are born until you take your last and final breath of this life.

Your body is your home, and she wants you to come back home!

Have you ever seen those dormant empty houses that just sit out in fields, falling down, neglected, vacant, uncared for?

Don't let your body become one of those buildings.
Don't let your body fall so far into disrepair, that it starts to let you down.
Don't care so little for your body, because one day, you will need her more than ever, and her wont be able to help you.

Your body, your one true home wants you to come back.

Your body is the chosen vessel of transportation for your soul throughout this life. You need to care, nurture and love this vessel or it may let you down.
You need to look through the panoramic viewing window and see life and all of its glory in widescreen, as a bigger picture.
Recognise the importance of your body and your mind combined.
YOU have a choice to either be a passenger in your chosen vessel, or you can choose to be the captain.
It is your choice, but you need to understand that any outcomes are the product of your decision, your actions and your choices.

Tune in to your body, come home to it and recognise it!

See the scars that tell your story!
Acknowledge the perfect imperfections, they are who you are!
Choose to listen, for that will take you to where you want to be!

Your body is priceless!
Your body is a masterpiece of evolution!
Your body is beautiful!
Your body is YOUR home! FOREVER!

Love her, nurture her, care for her and she will gift you the same privileges in return!

Stop worrying about what might not happen and start getting excited about would could happen!

Know Who You Are!

From the moment that we are born, we are subjected to influence. These influences shape who we are, what we feel, what we like, what we dislike and how we act and behave.

They are also heavily involved in how our habits form and develop over many years of our lives, maybe even our entire lifetime.

As children we are not led to believe that carbs are bad, we are not concerned about the sugar content of sweets, we are not manipulated to believe food is good or bad, we are not brought up to count calories. In fact, in most cases, we are simply told to eat all of our greens.

This obsession comes later on, as we move into teenage years or perhaps our early twenties. The media forcing us to look at highly airbrushed photographs of slim women looking amazing! Peer-pressure from our friends, siblings and colleagues and the *"Oh I wish I could look like her"* conversations that happen over our lunch break.

The "how to" columns in magazines that give us step by step instructions on how to achieve the celebrity look. Why do you need to look like another person anyway? You are not them, You are you. You are YOU-nique! You have your own "ism's" and shit to deal with.

Why should we obsess about looking like someone else?

Somewhere in amongst the screwed up-ness of all of these conversations, articles, columns and more, we suddenly find the need to live our lives by rules.

And these rules have given us the "control" that we needed, or at least so we thought!
These rules promised to make us look like a Hollywood A-Lister, or maybe even a reality show F-Lister. Either way, these rules have done nothing but cause us pain and disconnect.

I spoke earlier about trusting your body, trusting your gut feelings and recognising what your body is saying to you, telling you, asking you, and the truth is, when I have spoken about this during workshops, webinars, courses, coaching calls and just with friends, most women simply do not trust their bodies enough to let go.

They do not trust that they wont find themselves face down in a tub of cookie dough ice cream or box of chocolates.

We have this deep seated belief that if we are not "in control", not manipulating our meals, counting or tracking something, keeping a close eye on things, then we'll just binge all day every day on complete crap.

I thought this too, how can I NOT track, count, weigh, measure and so on, but the moment that I broke this relentless cycle of cray-cray habits and beliefs, something quite genuinely incredible happened.

I actually stopped eating shit! I stopped bingeing! I stopped craving junk! I stopped drinking fizzy drinks! I just stopped!

I tuned in to my body so much, that I started to notice things that I had ignored for years, maybe even decades.
I started to notice how foods made me feel, which foods made me feel great, which foods made me feel sluggish, which foods made my body skip with pleasure and which made me slump with lethargy.

I started to work with my body to give it all of the things that made me feel alive and in a very short space of time, my body, my food, my attitude and my life had made some very drastic changes....
But I hadn't even been trying.

There were no rules!

I never said that I couldn't have something, it was always there if I wanted it, but I just didn't want it!

We live in fear that without this control and all of the rules and restrictions of diets, we will fall apart, give up and gain more weight.

But you need to listen closely, listen to your body, hear your gut feelings and dial in to your intuitiveness.

Believe and trust in your body!

Ask yourself:

* Why do I need to be in control?
* What am I actually in control of?
* What is this control achieving for me?
* Am I really even in control?

The only reason you ever feel out of control, is because you are so regimented and strict on yourself to be in control. So if you removed the need for control, you would inevitably remove the feeling of being out of control!
You need to embrace the chaos of life, and be who you are meant to be, remove the influences and take back your life with all of its messy miraculousness.

Think about you, who you are, what you want and where you want to be.
Think about your future!
Think about your future self!
Think about your future body!

Step away from control and enjoy the rollercoaster that is life and the freedom that it offers.

Food is not the problem, it is just a symptom of your influences.

Think about it, did your parents ever say you could have dessert if you cleared your plate? This could have caused you to eat more than you needed and affected your recognition of fullness.
Did they ever give you sweets as a way to reward you for tidying your room? This could have created a behaviour that allows you to reward with food.
Did they make you eat foods that you didn't really enjoy eating? This could have led you to believing that you don't like a certain food, just because of the rebellion that you felt towards eating it as a child.

Think about all of the food related instances in your childhood, and then think about how they may have affected and influenced you, think about how you act with food now.

Are they linked?
How are they linked?

Your behaviour as an adult could potentially be an act of rebellion against your parents.
But the thing is, you are no longer a child.
You need to step away from rules, step away from influence, step away from control and let food be thy medicine!

Give in to your body, surrender and let go of control!

The moment of surrender is not when life is over. It's when it begins!

Marianne Williamson

Are We There Yet?

You know, every time that you step on to the scales, it's basically the equivalent of that back seat holla *"are we there yet?"*.

Deep down, you know that nothing has really changed since you last weighed yourself, less than 24 hours ago, yet you still tip toe on to the scales and cross your fingers, hoping for some kind of miraculous over night result.

But, even if you had lost a pound, maybe even two, what does it really show you?
Maybe you have just been to the loo and got rid of some excess waste - hmm yeah - I am talking about you emptying your bowels. We all do it, and yes, it can show a weight difference, up to 3lbs in fact.
Hoorah!!!

NO!
Not hoorah, going to the toilet is not a weight loss method.
It's a natural thing that SHOULD be happening on a daily basis. Not something to use as a measure of how much weight you have lost.

And, even if there is no movement from that needle (*fuck you scales*), It's just another rule that will cause you pain, and what is all of it really achieving, and what is it actually stopping you from doing?

NOTHING!

So many times over the past decade, probably longer, I have heard the sentence that starts with "When I...."

"When I have lost the weight, I will…"
"When I am 5lbs lighter, I will…."
"When I can get in my size 10 jeans, I will…."

But why wait?
Why are you putting your life on hold for the sake of a few pounds?
Why deprive yourself of fun, experiences, events, memories, when you could be out there living and enjoying them today?

I talked about the rules and restrictions that 'diets' put on us, but what about the rules and restrictions that we put upon ourselves?
It is basically the same principle.

DEPRIVATION!

Throughout my career, I have asked the question "Why?" To so many women:

Why do you want to achieve that?

And in the majority of situations, the answer has been one of a few things:

"I want to lose a few pounds for my holiday!"
"I want to be in good shape for my wedding!"
"I want to look good naked!"
"I want to be fit and fabulous at 40, 50, 60 etc!"

All valid reasons that I am sure many women can, and will relate to.

But, did you achieve it?
If you did, well done. Did you maintain it?
If you didn't, why not? What stopped you?

In the first instance, you may not have improved your mindset, you probably didn't acknowledge, accept or heal your root pain that has been causing your poor eating habits and behaviours, but we've already covered that.

So, in the second instance, ask yourself if you were chasing the right goal?
Were you chasing the goal for the right reasons?
Was the goal, and your reasons even your own, or a product of the influences that you have faced?

When I dig a little deeper with some of the Goddess Lifestyle clients, and really uncovered their reasons, it often turns out, what they were chasing wasn't what they want at all.
It wasn't their own goal!
It was what they "thought" would make them happy.
What they thought people expected of them!
It wasn't actually what they wanted!
Not even close!

When we start to focus on our own mindset, our own relationship with our self, our body, our mind and with our food, other relationships begin to change.

Relationships that may have otherwise just been left to stagnate, tick-over or run themselves.
These relationships with our friends, family members, colleagues, even our partners and children start to flourish.
The real you has come out to shine, and shiny things attract other shiny things. In other words, positivity breeds positivity, love breeds love, happiness breeds happiness.

Our efforts in our own relationship transcends in to those around us, in to the people we spend the most time with, the people we care about, lifting these relationships to new, beautiful and sometimes dizzying heights.

Ever heard an older couple say that they have fallen in love with each other all over again?
Normally this suggests that one has found contentment or happiness somewhere else in their life, or in their relationship with themselves, allowing a new, more vibrant side of their being to shine.

These relationships can push us to do more, see more, feel more and heal more. They push us to love more!

Laughter really can be the best medicine!

So, when I talk to women about their desires, their body goals, their health and lifestyle ambitions, the question is no longer "Why do you want to achieve this?"

No, now instead I ask:

What would this give you?
What would this bring to your life?
How would this help you to love yourself more?
How would this make you feel?
Why is this so important to you?

The series of 5 questions ultimately helps to build a picture of your future self, allowing you to see and feel the reason that you want to change. Allowing you to see your true goal.

BUT, no amount of seeing your future self will fix your inner self if you do not spend some time healing your root pains and your inner hurts.
You need to spend time with this and find your answers.

If you have ever said that you want to lose weight for a holiday (*and have't we all*), then the all of the attempts and efforts that you put in, may have be in vain.

Your holiday was already booked, right?

Whether you lost the weight or not, you would still go on holiday, correct?

Would the fact that you didn't achieve your dress size or perfect weight, really change the holiday?

No, of course not!
Regardless of your achievements, you would still go on holiday and you would still have a great time.

And, even if you had achieved it, what would really be different?

You may still have hang ups about your body, because like I said at the beginning of this book, you will not find happiness in a dress size or weight.

And even if you achieved your goal dress size or weight, would that immediately release you from all of the controlling mind games of diets?
Would you suddenly be free from rules and restrictions? Or would you be watching everything that you ate and drank whilst on holiday, or be planning to hit another new diet as soon as you got back?

This is all of the work that needs to be going on inside of your own mind, loving your body, loving yourself and loving your food so it can love you in return.

You wont find happiness in a bikini! In fact, back when I was a size 8, I felt worse in a bikini than I do now.

I felt like EVERYONE was judging me, critiquing my body, analysing my flaws, laughing at my cellulite and so on.

That was a tough place to be! Hey, hand me my cover up please!

Ii I'm honest, the reason that you had set the goal is not really that important, least of all to you.
If it was, you would have achieved happiness a long time ago!

Having a holiday body just ain't that important!
It isn't your real goal!

My point here is don't waste your life chasing numbers.

Live your life with happiness and love, and your body will find its own way to a happy place that you can both enjoy. A place where you, your mind and your body can all live harmoniously together, forever - happy!

Don't chase a false dream hoping to find your 'happy-ever-after' - I hate to say this, but it is a bit like the pot of gold at the end of a rainbow, or finding a unicorn or seeing the tooth fairy.
As mystical and luring as all of these things may be, they are all myths (sorry if you still believe in the tooth fairy!).

Think about it, how many women do you know that have achieved a weight loss or reached their perfect size?

Of these women, how many have gone on to live "happily-ever-after"?

How many of these women are still "dieting" to maintain, or relapsing, or yo-yo-ing, or chasing the next goal?

Fix your hurts, resolve your pains, create the loving mindset and live a life of love and happiness - that is where you will find your 'happily-ever-after'.

Only when you realise that happiness comes from within, will you be able to move away from the "perfect 10", the diet lifestyle, the yo-yo culture and move forwards with your life confidently.

Let go of labels, pigeon holes, boxes, rules, diets and goals.

Live a life of freedom, of love, of gratitude and allow yourself and your body time to find peace - your real happy place.

Happiness comes from within, it cannot be forced and it certainly cannot be faked.

Believe me!

I have starved myself in secret, I have restricted myself, I have taken pills, potions, shakes and laxatives, anything to weigh my "goal" weight, or to fit in to a bikini.

And even when I have got there, when I have achieved it and succeeded at any cost (usually my own health and energy) guess what...
I would look in the mirror and turn away - I still wouldn't be happy.
A few more pounds, another inch. I would still want more. I would always want more!
To lose more, to weigh less, to have tighter abs or firmer thighs.
To have less cellulite or smaller love handles.

When does it actually stop...?
Perfection?
There is no such thing!

The actual moment that it all stops, is when you stop harming yourself trying, and start loving yourself.

When you love your body and mind enough that your imperfections become perfections.

When you stop worrying about what complete strangers might think, and start embracing just how beautiful you and your body really are.

Only when you find peace with yourself and your body and your food, only then will this acceptable form of self harm come to an end.

To answer the title question, Are we there yet?

The answer lies within your relationship, not just with yourself, but with your thoughts, your mind, your body and your food.

Heal your internal pains and find peace.

Find happiness from inside, and recognise that you're beautiful, you are an amazing and strong women, embrace your self, love yourself and heal yourself.

Start to give a shit!

True Healing will always begin with your thoughts. Master your thoughts and you will master your life.

April Peerless

Macros This! Calories That! WTF?

In all of the years that I have worked in the fitness industry, and all of the various "nutrition" modules, courses and workshops that I have attended, not one has ever really honestly scratched the surface, Nutrition is such a huge subject, and a confusing one at that, so I decided to go back to school and learn the REAL crux for food, what is true and what is complete BS.

For maybe six out of eleven years, I was probably just as confused as the rest of the world.
The whole clean eating, low carb, sugar free, macro tracking, intermittent fasting lifestyle, day after day, question after question, which diet is best….
It was all just a little bit of an overload!

Like you, I would swap from one diet to another, from this plan to that plan, this cleanse to that cleanse, I mean, one of these has gotta work, right?

- Cut our gluten.
- Cut out dairy.
- Cut out sugar.
- Cut out cooked foods.
- Cut out processed foods.
- Cut out foods with added flavour.
- Cut out foods with 0% fat.

O.M.G!

- You can only eat between 4pm and 7pm.
- You can't have any carbs after 5pm.
- You can only drink tea on Sundays.

- You can only have chocolate on Wednesday, between 5.45 and 6pm and only if the sun is shining.
- You can only have decaf coffee.
    - No scrap that, you should never have decaf coffee!
    - Wait what? No coffee at all?
- You can only steam your veggies, but not for too long, you'll kill off all the good nutrients.
    - Actually, no you should boil them.
    - Hang on, wait, is it better to fry them... oh who really bloody knows!
- You shouldn't eat red meat. But now you're low on protein.
- You can only have a shake for breakfast.
- You can only eat boiled chicken.
- You can only eat vegetable.
    - But not potatoes, they are too starchy.
    - But what about sweet potatoes?
- You need to eat more protein, but you should still avoid red meat.
- You can only eat organic foods.
- You should watch out for BPA in packaging.
    - Better be safe and not eat any packaged foods, just in case.
- You should only have lactose free milk, just in case your allergic.
    - Better still cut out dairy and all of its imitations.
- You should avoid fat, unless it is good fat, but still not too much, it is still fat!
- Don't eat sugar.
    - Only natural sugar, but wait, thats still sugar, the body doesn't know the difference, better just avoid all fruit as well.

High fat - Low carb

High carb - Low fat
Low fat - Low carb
Paleo, Atkins, 5:2, Dukan, Vegan, IIFYM, Raw, Clean...

SERIOUSLY!!! STOP!!! PLEASE!!!

Is this normal? Sensible? Natural?

Is it any wonder that we are all so screwed up about food and our relationship with it?

There surely must come a point, where all of this information will overload and overwhelm us so much that we will just stop eating altogether!

Anyone fancy one of those sticks of gum from Willy Wonka's factory. You know the one that was three meals in one! Done! That's that sorted, right?

Chances are that you have tried one of these *"rules"*, maybe two, three or even all of them.
Chances are that you tried really hard to stick with it for a while, but then... wagon, track, cliff, BANG!

Maybe you have looked in to these diets, got so confused and overwhelmed with all of the rules, that you just didn't bother trying.
Either way these diets, these rules, these conditions and restrictions have left you so disconnected, so bamboozled, so unsure, that the very thought of them sends you into a head-spinning, whirlwind of hot mess.

Cue face in pillow - screaming loudly!

The rule book - calories this, macros that!
Eat X, Y, Z, don't eat A, B, C!

Technically, all diets have their place in society, they work short term to give use one thing, but not the thing that we actually want - they don't give us long term happiness.

No! Diets work only to give us the sense of control that we have come to crave.

They all "technically" promote the same message as well - reduce crap, eat less, move more.

But, this formula isn't as straight forward as that, and you are probably well aware that not enough food is just as bad as too much food.

Ha-darn-it! Why can't this be simpler!

This is why you need to break free from the dieting mentality. It's a trap!

Be different and go against the grain, go in the opposite direction to everyone else.
Don't be an "ant" and just follow the crowd!
Go left, not right!
Go paradoxical!
Go anti-diet!
Rip up the rule book and skip freely into the sunset laughing uncontrollably.

I remember a while back one of my coaches said something to me, actually two things.
The first was make everyday an opposite day, do the opposite to your normal every day habits.
The second, life isn't meant to be so black and white, paint by numbers and live vibrantly!

The second one has always stayed with me, I literally do feel as though I walk around in my life painting by glorious numbers with glorious colours.
And you should too!

BREAK FREE! PAINT BY NUMBERS! LIVE!

The purpose of life is to live, to taste experience to the utmost, to reach out eagerly and without fear for newer and richer experience.

Eleanor Roosevelt

The Computer Says No!

Yeah, we are still talking about "diets".
I know, right?
Come on, how do I hear and heal?
All in good time my little padewans! All in good time!

If I am honest, I cannot say this enough.

For years, maybe even decades, you have followed the crowd, hopping from one diet to another to another, being let down, hurt, beaten down and lied to.
It will take more than just a few words typed on a page to change this mentality.
It takes you to believe and have faith, to take that step from serial dieter to rebel rule breaker!

Some of you will put this book down and transform almost instantly, others will take a little more convincing, but that's OK.
If we all just did the same thing, thought the same thing, life would offer no excitement!

Changing your habits can be challenging, changing the mindset that you have had for the last 10, 20, 30 maybe even 40 years, well that's another game altogether.

But as you read more and more of this book, as you listen more and more to your body, you will start to figure it all out, in your own time, at your own pace, in your own way.

There is no right or wrong, as long as you are listening and feeling! That's the truth!

Every diet EVER, has only ever served to deny you of something. Some diets even go as far as to deny you of everything.
Just think of juice cleanses, water diets, shakes, pills, potions, ancient Chinese remedies, fat burning coffees and secret ingredient sachets.

We've all seen them, maybe even been lured by their promises and tried them. I know I have fallen for them hook, line and sinker before.

Detox teas and skinny coffees, darn, what was I thinking?

Yeah, I admit to it, I've been there too!

Caffeine raises our metabolism.
Green tea raises our metabolism.
Ginseng, guarana, green tea extract, green coffee beans, the list goes on and on and on, and the manufacturers, much like the diet industry, know exactly how to market to your vulnerabilities, your pains and your weaknesses.

Drop a dress size in a week!
Lose 10lbs in 10 days!
Get flat abs in 30 days!

Blah, blah, blah.

And then, ha, then there is their social media campaigns.
You only need to spend a few minutes on any of the platforms to see that all of these photos are staged, sponsored or photoshopped. Or all three!

I mean, it wouldn't serve them well if they had someone less acceptably *"perfect"*, someone "normal" advertised their products.
Would it?

And hey, isn't that size-ism?

Pah, no thank you!
I am not falling for it any more!
Photoshopped, staged, perfectly lit photos in a kitchen that looks more like a show home than a real "lived in" kitchen!
Uh-uh, nope!
Give me real life any day!

These huge international companies are all scrambling for your money, your hard earned cash, and they are getting it. Millions and millions of pounds and dollars of it!
These companies, and the whole industry have very specific and targeted methods of advertising.
They know how to use trigger words, they know how to make you feel your root pain, they know how to make you feel urgency, desperation and not good enough, and they take advantage of this in broad day light.

Are you feeling abused yet?

They know how to tap in to your fragile relationship with food and your body, and they exploit it for profit.
BASTARDS!

So many social media accounts are sponsored, video channels used as an advertising platform and blogs reduced to product placement campaigns, just to get in front of you.
The consumer!

These advertising campaign are specifically designed to make you feel inadequate, worthless, hurt, sad and not good enough.
They make you feel worse.
Just so they can build you up and make you feel as though their product is the best, and only option.
Just so you part with some of that money in your pocket in the hope that this product will work.
Which it wont!

Happiness cannot be purchased in a bottle, neither can confidence or freedom or love. They are a product of your own mindset.

So please, don't be fooled by big promises and shiny pink labels. They are just rules in disguise, masquerading as hope, and they will let you down and fail you. Just like the diets did!

––––––––––––––

DENIAL!

If I said to you right now that you couldn't eat any chocolate for the rest of this week, what do you think would happen?

You immediately fixate on the one thing you are being denied of! You focus on the negative.

Have you ever been scheduled in for surgery?
Your consultant and nurses have told you that you cannot eat or drink for a certain amount of time prior to the procedure.

You go to bed the night before feeling fine, if not a little anxious and nervous. But the next morning when you wake, despite the fact that you have skipped breakfast for the past five years, you suddenly can only think about how hungry you are and that you want breakfast.

You can only focus on what you are not allowed.
You focus on the denial!

A diet plays out in the same way, we always focus on what we can't have, rather than all of the wonderful things that we can have.

We only see the "downside", the rule itself.

Effectively, we only hear the diet saying NO!

No carbs, no bread, no cheese, no milk, no sugar, no coffee, no cake, no dairy, no fizzy drinks, no gluten, no fat, no alcohol, no, no, no, no, no, no, no, no, no, no, NO!

When I start coaching a new client, I ask them to STOP dieting and START thinking!

Thinking about all of the foods that they CAN have, the tastes, the textures, the feelings, the experiences.
I ask them to take their time with food and consider what the food is to them, what it is doing for them and what it is doing for their body.

I challenge you to do the same, to start thinking about all of the wonderful foods that are available to you, and all of the wonderful and loving foods that you should be feeding your body with… just think of all of that love that you could be having?

When we "diet", we do not just deprive ourselves of nutrients, tastes, textures.
No, we deprive our lives.

We are held down by ball and chain, shackled to a life that is far less fun and enjoyable than that of someone who doesn't diet. Someone who is not bound by rules.

The diet tells us that we cannot go for afternoon tea with our gorgeous mum, the calories don't fit!

We cannot go for coffee with the girls, there might be cake there and we can't control our temptation and desire.

We can't go on a dinner date with Mr Sexy Pants, because we may lose control, binge and destroy the dessert cart... (Oh the shame, what would he think of me!)

I better just avoid all of these experiences, so that I can stay in control... so I don't binge on all the things that I CAN'T have!

We don't just deprive ourselves, our lives and our bodies, we also deprive the people around us that we love or perhaps, maybe would like to love.

We cannot be ourselves, we cannot be true to our self or to our friends, we are shackled by rules.
We cannot live our fullest life!!!

Think about it, how many things have you missed out on because of the words "I am on a diet!"

How many memories have you not made because of the words "I am on a diet!"

How many awesome days or nights out with friends have you been missing from, because of the words "I am on a diet!"

How many Mr Sexy Pants have you missed out on, because of the words "I am on a diet!"

Honestly, our lives would be so much more colourful, enjoyable, richer, happier, more fulfilling and more exciting if it wasn't for the diet!
We would feel better, be better, we would be ourselves!

Diets just tell you NO!

Release yourself from the rules and start enjoying your life. I can promise you that you will very quickly start to notice how different you feel.

*If you obey all of the rules,
you will miss all of the fun!*

Scrutiny Mutiny

I have spoken to women who have gone as far as to remove all mirrors from their home, or at least full length mirrors. But this is crazy!

This is a very extreme form of self loathing behaviour that has been created, fuelled and driven by your negative relationship with your body, your food and your thoughts.

This NEEDS to change!

One of the most important things that you need to firstly notice, and prevent yourself from doing is scrutinising every single inch of your body!
Stop beating her up and abusing her emotional and verbally.

Your body hears everything that you and your mind thinks, even those internal whispers!

Notice your self talk, your internal monologue, and start to create a more positively affirming conversation with yourself.

Start to listen up! Start to hear! Start to feel!

Start to notice how your body feels, and focus on the positives, start to praise and thank her, be grateful to her and be grateful FOR her.
She is trying to look after you!

Hearing, and even listening can feel challenging to begin with, but persevere, she will talk to you.

Sooner or later, you will hear her and you will instinctively recognise what she is saying.
Sit up and pay attention!

I think back to when I attended a three day seminar in London. It was three days of intensive mindset coaching and self love.

We spent the best part of an entire afternoon just looking at our reflections in the mirror *(and yes, back then it was a very uneasy experience)*.

The exercise is designed to bring home just how uncomfortable you feel in the most important relationship you can have. The one between you and your body.
It made you notice your discomfort with yourself, your body, your person!

Many of us struggled to look into our own eyes, let alone speak to, listen to or hear our own bodies.

We needed to forgive!
We needed to reconnect!
We needed to find peace and we needed to find love.

Try it!

Find a mirror and look into your own eyes.
Feel the relationship between you and yourself.
How happy is this relationship?
If this was a relationship with another person, how would it make you feel?

Try and FEEL yourself, feel your hurts, your pains, your questions, your resentments.

Try and feel all of the emotions, all of the good, the bad and the ugly.
Find your pain and sit with it for a while.
Listen to it, counsel yourself and see what answers you can find.

Take your time!
Take it slowly!
One step, one pain, one moment at a time!

Try and find your release, your forgiveness, your inner peace!

We all need to let our barriers down and allow ourselves to come back to our body, come home to her. Allow the love to flood in, or even just trickle in to start with, that would be a damn good start.

Take some time out to spend with yourself, your body, your mind, look in the mirror and start to use that big paint by numbers brush.
Start to notice all of the positives, no matter how big or small they may be.

Start to paint love and life on all of the gloriously beautiful things about your body and you!

When you are ready, and only when you are ready, look deep in to your own eyes and talk to your soul!
Talk to your body!
Talk to your mind!
Talk to you!
Speak from the heart and speak with love!

Feel! Love! Care! Nurture!

Reconnect with your body, start to rebuild the bond and start to feel love. Whether it's a drip, a trickle or a pour, just start to let love back in!

Start to break down those shackles that have bound you for so long and walk freely into tomorrow, the next day, the next day and the next.

Start to live a pure and loving life of freedom and light, of self embracing love and kindness.

The Start of a new chapter in your life, starts when you turn to a new page!

*Watch carefully the magic that
occurs, When you give a person
just enough comfort,
to be themselves.*

Atticus

A Declaration of Love

I am a beautiful human being.
I feel a loving bond with my body, and connect with her every day.
I listen to her, hear her, feel her and respect her.
I do not feel guilt for my food choices, nor do I hold on to them.
I slow down for me and my body, and feed us both with the loving and nurturing thoughts and foods that serve us and our future self.
I have a life of abundance, and an abundance of love for myself, my body and for others.
I am the queen of my destiny and the ruler of my thoughts.
I treat my body like she is my best friend. She is my best friend.
I enjoy living a life of freedom, love and beauty.
I forgive myself for any past decisions that did not honour or serve me or my body.
I know that by expressing my own positivity, I share this with the world, and the world will share back more of the same.
I share my smile with the universe, so that the universe can smile back at me.
I do not allow myself to succumb to the control of diets, the rules, the scales or the numbers. I care only for feelings.
I make myself my priority.
I love myself, my body and my mind!
I am an amazing human being!

What a wonderful thought,
that some of the best days of
our lives are yet to come.

Let's Make Up & Be Friends

Remember when you were younger, when you and your best friend would fall out at school, usually over something really small (*often a boy, I bet?*).
Do you remember when you would make up?

Or maybe when you and your partner have had a fight and you didn't talk for a few days, but then would have amazing make up sex?

Do you remember how exciting it felt to make up?
How happy it made you feel?

Imagine how it would feel to make up with someone that you haven't really paid attention to for a number of years. Imagine how exciting and amazing it would feel to be back together.

It's time to make up ladies, and make up for good.

Your body is screaming for you to come back, to listen up, to feel her once again.
She wants you to come home and sit in front of a roasting open fire with a hot chocolate and talk all night long about anything and everything!
She just wants you home!

Earlier in the book I talked about your relationship with your food and your body, and how it would make you feel if this was a relationship with another person.
How would you feel if someone was constantly abusing you, demeaning you, bitching about you, saying horrible things about you?

How would you react?

Understanding your relationship with yourself is the first step to healing that relationship.

I always think that it is best to understand where you start from, before you try and tackle where you want to get to. I apply this same method in my coaching.

If you haven't already sat and thought about your relationship with food and how this is guiding your relationship with your body, and vice versa, then spend some time with it now.

Finish this chapter, put the book down and sit with it.

How is your relationship?

Is it excessive, guarded, restrained, secretive, addictive or controlled?
Is it pleasurable or painful?
Abusive or violent?
Is it boring, placid, uneventful, uninspiring or lacking fun and adventure?

Consider this, if you were to talk to your mum, your siblings or girlfriends about this love affair, this relationship, would they be happy for you?
Would they support it or would they urge you to get out?
Would your dad, or your brother be doing the over-protective thing that they do?

Does this relationship leave you feeling good, happy, excited or does it leave you feeling neglected, unloved and unimportant?

Is it lacking something that would lead you to spending your weekends engaged in debaucherous shenanigans that ended in you feeling guilt, hiding more secrets and suppressing out-of-control desires and cravings?

Does this relationship make you feel happy?
Are you satisfied, satiated and content?

Is it a rocky road of love and hate that is riddled with confusing highs and lows?
Are you fighting urges, thoughts and secret rendezvous?
Are you in control or are you being controlled?

There are so many questions and so many ways to take stock of your current relationship, but you need to see how your love affair with food is affecting your relationship with yourself and with your body!

How much can your body take?
How much can YOU take?

It comes back to the need to feel *"in control"*.
But this need for control fuels the feeling of being out of control.
So we need to remove the problem of control in order to remedy the symptom of feeling out of control.

BREAK FREE!

When I think back to that first reiki healing, that first moment of trying to reconnect with myself, the healer told me that I had lost connection with myself, with my femininity.
This made sense to me, I didn't feel *"girly"*, I didn't feel *"me"*.

I had lost my way amidst all of the internal bullshit that I had been loading myself up with.
Rules, restrictions, internal arguments.

But, gradually, through taking the time to listen to my body, heal my mind and nurture myself, I was able to reconnect.
I was able to find love for myself and respect for my body.
I was able to love my body, and all of its scars.

This led to something quite beautiful.
I felt balanced!
With equal doses of fun, excitement, love, compassion, self worth and girly-ness.
I wiped out all of my hurts.
I healed!
I found my home, my heart and my self all in the same place at the same time, like three best friends having a coffee - togetherness!

I had made up with my body and she had made up with me.
We stopped fighting, arguing, battling against each other.
The more love I gave her, the more she gave me.
The more I nurtured her, the more she nurtured me.
The more she told me, the more I could tell her.
This is a friendship that would only blossom bigger and stronger as time passed by.

By finding love for my body, I wanted to nurture her, I wanted to feed her, I wanted to look after her and look out for her.
This meant feeding her with all of the best and most loving foods.

By healing my relationship with my body, I healed my relationship with food. By healing my relationship with food, I healed my relationship with my mind.

Having this love in my life, gave me more than just balance and happiness, it gave me my life back. I suddenly had time for me, for the things I loved and the people I loved.

Positivity breeds positivity!

What you give, you get back!

With the improvement of the relationship I had with myself, came the improvement of my relationship with others.
I felt a warm and fuzzy feeling, which I had long forgotten existed, I felt love and received love in return.

I urge you to heal your relationships, make up with yourself, your body and your food and watch your life light up.

What if you simply devoted this year to loving yourself more?

Find Your Reason

- Why do you want to change?
- Why are you not beautiful the way you are?
- Why are you unhappy?
- What are you unhappy about?
- Why haven't you changed yet?

There is always an excuse why we haven't done something yet, why we didn't quite get there or simply didn't try, and part of the problem is that we do not recognise the *"why"*.

I spoke about this a little bit before, knowing your reasons. But it's not just as simple as plucking it out of thin air and just getting on with it, like I said.

I spoke about how your holiday just wasn't important enough to inspire you, and I meant it.

Yes, I know that holidays are important, but they will come and they will go regardless of how we look or feel.

Over the years, I have encouraged my clients to find their *"why's"* in a more unique (*or should that be YOU-nique*) approach.
A journey into their own subconscious mind, into the past, present and forward to the future.
A journey of discovery and honest realisation.

Sometimes these methods provoke tears of joy, other times they provoke tears of pain, but these tears are crucial, as they unlock something that we all have, deep inside of us, deep, deep down, almost forgotten about.

These tears reawaken your inspiration.

You see, you can be motivated by seeing someone else do or achieve something, it kind of lets us know that it is possible. But motivation doesn't connect with you, it doesn't connect with your emotions and it doesn't connect with anything that you hold important.

Motivation may get you started, but it will not keep you going - ergo - track, wagon, cliff, bang!

In order to find your true reason, you need to connect the love, the emotion, the future, the past. A bit like connecting the dots on a childs puzzle.
You need to open your heart and let love and emotion inspire you.

Think of it like this, imagine one of those old telephone exchanges, you know, the ones with all of the wires that the operator had to plug and unplug to connect the caller.
That's what you need to do now, you need to connect and reconnect your emotions to your future self in order to inspire the change itself.

Try looking at things from a different perspective, rather than focussing on what you want to change about yourself, focus on what you want to change about your life and your future.

Think about how changing you, would change that future, and not just your future, but the futures of all of the people whom you love, who are important to you.

Even if they are not around yet (*if you want children for example or haven't met Mr Sexy Pants yet!*).

How would changing YOU change certain aspects of your life? Your family, your love life, your children, your career, your happiness?

What would this change give to you and what would it give to those who you love?
What would it bring to your life?

Think into your future, visualise yourself five, ten, fifteen years from now, what do you have then, that you do not have right now?
How do you feel as your future self?
How does this make you feel now?
FEEL IT!
Is it a good feeling?
Grab hold of that emotion and keep hold it.

Think of the MUCH bigger picture!

If you want to, you can write down your reasons, your future, your changes.
Connect with them on a deeper level by committing them to paper or grab a journal and just write your thoughts and feelings down.
Perhaps doodle, scribble or draw them.
Colour them in, add vibrance, make them even more exciting and never stop dreaming.

Keep thinking!

I challenge you to think of as many reasons as possible.

And when you feel as though you can't think of any more, simply go back and think about each of the reasons you have already captured individually - what would that give you? What would it give to your closest and most important loved ones?

Every time one particular reason provokes an emotional response, whether it is deep belly laughter, tears or just humbling, highlight it.

That is a gorgeous gift from your subconscious, that is one of your most personal and important reasons.
Keep hold of it!
These reasons are what will inspire you to act.

Keep your reasons safe, private and in mind.
Keep the emotional attachment!
And continue to add to the list.
Keep growing your own personal bank account of inspiration.

Having done this exercise, having thought about your future and your personal reasons, you should no longer be that bothered about the holiday goal, you have much bigger and better aims. All of which connect to love, and will serve to help build that connection with yourself and create your future self in the process.

Let go of what is *"expected"* and go with what you love!

What is right for you! What is important to you!

GO WITH YOU!

Go confidently in the direction of your dreams. Live the life that you have imagined.

Be Reborn

You are you, but by repairing all of the damage and hurt in your relationship with yourself, you can be reborn as a brighter, shinier, happier you - the future you!

How exciting is that?

The possibilities for the future you are endless, but you will still be you, you cant change that, and why would you want to?

You are a gorgeous human being!

In the last chapter, I spoke about your reasons, your true, emotional, love felt and connected reasons.

These should have given you a greater insight of what your future could be, what your future self could be like.
There is nothing more exciting for me as a coach seeing my clients feel their own future and believing in it too.
The birth of the future you!

Sit quietly, alone and undisturbed and just think about YOUR future.

See it in your mind.
Meditate with it if you like.

See where you are, who you are with, what you are doing, what are you wearing, what you are talking about, how do you look, how are you feeling, what is your mood?

FEEL!

Feel the emotions that are attached to this future, take a mental photograph.

See it! Feel it! Believe it!

How does this make you feel?

Feel free to doodle, sketch, scribble or draw your future, make notes, keep it fresh and feel it regularly.

Visit the future you as often as you need to, meditate with her, and see if you can talk to her. Maybe write her a letter that she can read on a date that you set!

Allow the image of your future, the feelings that it brings, the emotions that you feel, guide you in healing your relationship with yourself, your body, your food today, tomorrow and the next day.

Allow this image to open you up to who you want to be.

Allow this image to take you on a journey of self love from this day onwards.

See it! Feel it! Believe it! Then take action to achieve it!

Love yourself as if you are already your future self, and you will, in time, become the future self that you have created.

Create Your Own Future

You are the queen of your own destiny, the ruler of your thoughts!
Pay attention and never stop listening.

Switch on to yourself, tune in to *"me.fm"* and see, hear and feel everything.

Ask yourself - does this "support" the future me?
Would the future me be grateful for this?
Does this serve me today for my future me tomorrow?

There is no scrutiny, judgement or controlling thoughts, only choices!

There is always a choice and that choice is always yours!

Is what I am doing today helping me to become the future self I want to be?

Own your actions, this is what you have chosen to do.
The person you want to be!
Don't judge, punish or get angry if things do not support the future.
Choose to accept, forgive and carry on.

Remember the next action will be for the future!

Slowly, slowly. One day, one moment at a time.

Take your time! Listen Up! Choose!

The best way to predict the future is to create it!

Peter F. Drucker

Who Said That? (Binge Bitch, Binge!)

We all have two sides, but that is not to say that we are all like Jekyll and Hyde, but we certainly do all have a nice and a naughty voice inside of our heads.
But we don't always acknowledge this, and that can cause us a few problems.

Some people refer to this *"other voice"* as the inner bitch, or the food monster, some call her the evil twin, but whatever you call her, however you acknowledge her, it is a big step in the right direction.

Earlier in the book I asked if you ever felt as though food is calling you from the fridge, luring you in to indulge, enjoy, binge.
And of course, we all know that food can't speak, so let's stop trying to pass blame onto inanimate objects.

NO!

This little voice that appears all dressed up like a chocolate cheesecake, that is the voice of your inner other.
And she is a little bit of a demon actually.

She isn't just responsible for the food-voices that you hear, but so much more.
She blurts out a lot of stuff, completely unbothered by how it makes you feel and regardless of how much it causes you to disconnect from your body.

She doesn't care if you feel pain, sadness, anguish, hurt, guilt, despair, heartache and disappointment.

Just think of all of those times that you have said:

"I am not good enough", that was her!
"I'll never achieve it!" That was her too.
"I wish I could…., but it's too hard!" Yep, all her!
"Just one more biscuit!" - her!
"You're so ugly, fat, unlovable, worthless, useless!" -

ALL HER!

Just think about all of the rules that you have tried to live by, abide by and broken. All of those diets, workouts, binges.
She has been in control for far too long and now it's time to shut her up!

I will be completely honest, you will never completely erase her from your mind, she will always be in there, she is, after all, part of you.
But by finding love for yourself, your body and your food, you will be able to put her on pause, mute her, or at the very least be able to hear her and recognise her as the devious and harming bitch that she is.

You will be able to override her and take back the driving seat of your own decisions. You will be the captain of your vessel once more!

The problem right now, is that she feeds off of your acceptance of her rule, and by believing what she is saying, you are only allowing her to take a tighter grip on your own reality.

So, start to listen out for her, your inner voice, and hear what she is saying.
Then, when you hear her, squash her down with all of that self love and self respect that you have been building up.

Lock her away in a dark corner of your mind and build her a little cell with all of the "me power" that you now have.

Tell her to be quiet and reaffirm your new found love for yourself.

Visualise it if you want, as this can help to strengthen the belief in this devious little character.

See her in the cell, see her quietly siting and sulking!

Don't allow her to ride on your shoulder any longer and lead you away from your own truth, your future you. Don't let her stop you from being excited about the new you, the loved you!

I will admit every now and then, she might slip out of her cell and do her best to catch you off guard, and if she does, don't worry.

It's ok!

Just breathe in love and light, own the action and move forwards with your head held high.

Put her back where she belongs, and be happy... You did a great thing there, because you noticed, you heard and you resolved. You stood up for yourself and your future self because you are feeling loved!

You are loving yourself more and more with each moment!

Keep going!

As I said earlier, so what if you ate something or maybe had a thought that doesn't support or serve the future you that you are living for.

That's ok!

As long as you recognised it and carried on without guilt or negativity.

It's just one thought out of a potential 75,000 thoughts that you might have that day.
And I think that you would agree, that is a much healthier and happier ratio than before, right?

Don't be angry with yourself or your body, don't try to punish or reprimand yourself.
That is the old you, who is still listening to the inner demon…. Get back to being the future you, that is where you belong!

Similarly, just because you hear that little voice calling out to you, doesn't mean that you need to listen.
That is YOUR choice!
Remember, you ALWAYS have a choice!
Just own your decisions!

Remember, this is your life, your body and your mind!
Love them and let them love you back!

Tell Your Tale

Food, glorious food!

Food is a beautiful thing!
Colourful, delicious, nourishing, loving, giving, kind and above all pleasurable.

I said earlier that food tells your story, your culture, your heritage and it does.
Across the world there are 7.6 BILLION people, all living very different lives, with very different tastes and very different food choices.

Out of all of those 7.6 BILLION people, there is only ONE of you!
There isn't anyone who is exactly like you!!!
Isn't that amazing!
There is only ONE YOU! One very special and beautiful you!

But how does food tell your beautiful story?
And what would your food story say about you?

I sometimes ask my clients *"If I had never spoken to you, or met with you, and you sent me an honest account of your food choices for 7-10 days, what would your food choices tell me about you?"*

- Would it tell me that you are a conscientious person who shops at a farmers market?
- Would it say that you grew up in a certain part of the world and follow a traditional diet?
- Would it tell me that you are scared of new or different foods?

- Would it say that you are not very skilled in the kitchen or lack cooking knowledge?
- Would it tell me that you are a bit of a *'foodie'* and you like swanky restaurants?
- Or perhaps it would tell me that you are past caring and just follow your inner demon.

Food is incredible, and how we think about it can often be very telling of our relationship with our body.

- Fresh food is so expensive, what's the point!
- I don't like X, Y, Z!
- I can't cook!
- I don't have time to cook!
- I don't understand whats good for me!
- I don't get food labels!
- I just don't know what I am doing anymore!

With the exception of the last three, most of these are simply excuses and really just say that you have disconnected from your body.
The last three tell me that you have been controlled by "diets" for so long that you have lost your way and do not know what to believe any more.

As I have said previously, just *"thinking"* about your food choices can dramatically change your relationship with food itself.

Try asking yourself some of these questions:

- What is this food to me?
- How does it make me feel?
- How does it make my body feel?
- Does it give me love and nourishment?
- Does it make me happy?
- Does it support the future me?

- Does it actually taste good?
- Can I chew it slowly and taste it?
- Does it make me feel any guilt?
- Does it suit the life that I want to live?
- Does it cause me physical or emotional pain?
- Do I enjoy it?
- How does it feel in my mouth?
- Where did it come from?
- Was it grown/raised or made?
- Does it fit in with my personal morals and beliefs?
- Do I find myself labelling it *"good"* or *"bad"*?

You can make up your own questions to suit you, make them relevant and personal.
Link them to your emotions and your future self.

But, the main point here is just to think and feel!

Copy Cats!

You can't copy anybody and end up with anything. If you copy, it means you're working without any real feeling.

Society tells us that so-and-so from such-and-such blockbuster movie lost two stone in a day following this meal plan and that workout.

Our friends tell us that Suzie in the office dropped four dress sizes in a month by not eating anything white, and check out Maria who looks ten years younger because she followed the meal plan in last months glossy fronted magazine.

Well, if it worked for them, then it'll work for me, right?

First we copy and then we compare and it is a dangerous road to self blame, self loathing and self defeat.

Don't be fooled!

Something I learnt a long time ago is that you should never follow in someone else footsteps - they are NOT walking the same path as you!

Their life is not like yours, their body is not like yours, their mind is not like yours and their destination is not like yours!
They are not you, so why try to be them!

What works for one may not necessarily work for another, we are all unique and we all have very different lives and needs.

But, in many cases, we still do it anyway, we still copy, we still follow and we fall into the comparison trap.

When we compare things get a bit messy, not just because our results do not match theirs, not even close. But we begin to feel as though we have failed and when we fail, we fall.
When we fall, we binge.
When we binge, we abuse.

We fuel the pattern of rules and restrictions and begin to self-loath and push ourselves further into the luring promises of the diet culture.

We bounce back in a more extreme attempt and repeat the whole viscous cycle again.

It's painful!

There is no comparison!

You shouldn't even be comparing yourself to yourself!
I know that sounds crazy, but I have heard it so many times... *"When I was 20....!"*

This just leaves me with the heart breaking task of reminding my client that she is not 20 any more, she is in fact 40, 50, maybe even 60 years old.
Her body has changed, been through things, slowed down.

She may have had children, suffered an illness, received some kind of hormone treatment or other medication that could have changed how her body operates, and at what speed.
Our bodies changes as we age, just like us!

This is why is is so important to listen to your body, because she knows what she needs, what will make her feel better, work better, function better.
She knows!

Moving forwards into your future self, your future happiness, I have a saying, it's a bit of a mantra:

"Today, I will love more than I did yesterday, but not as much as I will tomorrow!"

Take each step of your transformation at a time, one foot in front of the other, one day after another.
Baby steps in the right direction are so much better than giant leaps that zig zag all over the place.

There is little point in biting off more than you can chew, I mean, technically, this is why we are all here in the first place.

No copying!
No comparisons!

You are YOU and YOU are you-nique!

Don't compare your life to others.
There's no comparison between the sun and the moon.
They both shine when it is their time.

The Real Stories

Social media has a lot to answer for!

The cyber world and it's constant spewing of fake stories only serves to fuel our own feelings of inadequacy.

Personally, I really do not feel much affection for social media sites, yes I use them to stay in contact with my amazing clients, but rarely do I share my personal life.

That's not because I am embarrassed, ashamed or scared, but because I am simply too busy enjoying the moments, enjoying my life and enjoying making the memories.

In fact, most of the times and experiences that I would happily share, I am so lost in the moment that my phone stays firmly in my pocket or handbag.
I simply forget to hashtag that moment, because I am happy within it.

I was talking to a friend of mine who works in a similar field to myself, this friend shares literally every moment, and for this reason she has tens of thousands of followers.
But she opened up to me and told me that for every picture that she shares, there is sometimes up to sixty other attempts that she has deleted.

She said that when she hashtags food images, by the time she actually starts to eat, the food is often cold.
And any images of her body can take anything up to forty minutes to capture just one photo.
She wont post unless it is perfect!

The one thing that I really got from this conversation was the pressure that she felt to be perfect.
To live the perfect life, have the perfect moments and the perfect smile, and body, ALL of the time.
Just like I use to!

She is too busy trying to share her moments, that she forgets to live within them, enjoy them and remember them.

Surely that is not a happy way to live?

I do understand how she feels though.
I use to apply the same pressures to my own social media images.
That was until I realised that you are basically flogging a false expectation, and further fuelling the pressures that both you and others feel to meet this cray-cray high expectation.

The lives that you see playing out in front of you on social media sites are often, I'm sad to say, not real!

You do not see the true stories behind the camera, or get to know the true person in the images.
You see the big, perfect smiles and the amazing friends, but you do not see how alone this person really feels, how unhappy they may be, how scared, tired or jaded they are.
You do not see how critical they are of themselves, their lives and their bodies.
You do not see them pinching their almost non-existent rolls of fat, whilst stepping on the scales or starving themselves.
You do not see the binges, the tears, the self loathing.

All you see is the big smiles and amazing friends.

Wow, she looks so happy! I bet she has the best life!

Sadly, all these people are doing is creating an alternative lifestyle, one that portrays perfection, one that makes them feel a little better, and one that sets the bar so high, that others feel as though this is the holy land, the secret kingdom and the hidden realm of happiness.

If I copy her, I can live like that.... right?

Stop believing in the hypocrisy of it all and start to follow real women leading real lives.
Women who eat greasy cheeseburgers and drink wine.
Women who skip the gym and watch a chick-flick instead.
Women who haven't done their make up, because they haven't had time!
Women who screw up and accept it!
Women who have a REAL life with REAL problems and REAL crap.

You may not be able to look for the truth in everyones story, or see what goes on behind the camera, but be realistic.
Is anyones life that completely perfect?

These women are often the lady we saw at the beginning of the book.
She was clothes shopping, remember?
Forced external confidence, trapped by their own expectations of what others expect of them.
I've been there, and it is a seriously lonely place.
Seek the Truth!
Seek the happiness!
Seek Authenticity!

We have to dare to be ourselves,
however frightening or strange
that self may prove to be.

May Sarton

Softly Softly

One of the biggest messages that I try to send out to my clients is to be gentle with yourself.
Be kind!
We are all too quick to get angry, frustrated, obsessed and bored, that we bully and beat ourselves.

If you eat the wrong things you feel angry with yourself.
If your body feels pain you feel frustrated with it.
If your mind tells you something you feel hurt or pained by it.

It's always a negative experience, but what about food?

Food is also treating our bodies harshly. Well, certain types of food at least!

Could our foods be kinder, gentler, softer?

Let's talk about food, and your relationship with it, or more specifically, your bodies relationship with it.

You see, we have talked about your relationship with food, yourself and your body, but what about the other relationship?
The one that goes on between your body and food?

Have you been noticing that?

Food feeds us with love! Have you felt it yet?

Truth is, we don't really pay much attention to what our food actually does for our body.

In fact, we are pretty misguided and unaware of what we are even putting into our bodies - as long as the calories fit, right?

WRONG!

I gave up calorie counting a long time ago, and it was around the same time that I started paying attention to what was IN food.
I started to listen and feel and love.
I started buying more fresh locally grown produce from a local farm shop and I started to understand what food was doing for me.
I started to notice how bad I felt when I was feeding myself with all of the chemicals, additives, flavouring and pesticides.
So, I took away a lot of the man-made trash that was causing me to disconnect from my body.

I am not telling you that you need to support your local famers and buy all organic foods that have been lovingly hand picked by cabbage patch kids.
And I am not saying that you need to remove anything from your shopping list.
All I am telling you is how I felt making this simple change.

And it is up to YOU to feel your body and how your body reacts to the foods that you are offering. This is why I say that you need to reconnect with your body and feel what she is telling you.

Within a very short space of time, I could see and feel the difference in my body, by nurturing and loving my body with a more nourishing and better quality foods, I noticed my stomach shrink!
My body felt good!

My body worked better!
I had more "ooomph"!

I FELT GOOD!

But why? My weight never changed a single pound!

One theory that I truly believe in, is that by reducing the amount of chemicals entering my body, I removed what had been irritating my insides for a very long time.
These chemicals had been causing my stomach and intestines to inflamme, and now they were no longer in my system, the reduction in inflammation was physically visible!

I was feeding my body with nurturing and loving foods and in return, my body was loving those foods.
She was really happy, and this was how she as showing me!

Soon after, I started to do a little research of my own.

I discovered that certain hormones accelerate the growth of Endometriotic tissue.
These hormones are often found in food products, and were potentially increasing and exacerbating the symptoms of my endometriosis.
So, I listened to my body and I decided to remove the offending foods.

Within days, the changes had been incredible. I had so much energy, I had no headaches, I had an even flatter stomach, I felt incredible! I felt loved!

BUT... none of these changes were rules, they were my own personal choices with my own personal reasons.

I had decided that I didn't want to feel this way, so for me, that was enough to not want to eat these certain foods.

But that is me, that is me being kind to my body, that is me going softly softly and not blaming my body or the food.

I just listened.

For you it will be different, you will have your own symptoms to heal, and just by listening to your body, you will be able to instinctively know how to do this.

JUST LISTEN UP! FEEL YOUR WAY!

It's ok to eat foods that are not organic!
It's ok if you do not eat 100% perfect!
It's ok to have some processed foods!
It's ok to eat pasta and breads!

It is ok to do all of these things IF you decide that they are right for you.
THEY ARE NOT PART OF A DIET!

It's ok to do whatever you want, as long as you are happy with your choices, and aware of if, and how it supports your future self (or not).

THAT IS YOUR CHOICE!

I will be honest, it is impossible to follow rules, and when it comes to living a healthy lifestyle, it is more about your mindset than your food.

If you can accept one thing from this book, then I hope it is the acceptance that perfect really doesn't exist!

You cannot eat perfect food perfectly ALL of the time.

In addition, as I have already said, you should not be following in the foot steps of any one else, they are not travelling the same path as you.

This is why when I coach people with their nutrition, I follow everything that I am telling you in this book.

LISTEN!
LEARN!
LOVE!

FUD

What is FUD?

**FEAR
UNCERTAINTY
DOUBT**

I am too old for street talk, there is all of these acronyms and abbreviations, and I will be honest, I get messages sometimes and I have to do an internet search on what they actually mean. Oh the shame! *lol* I am no longer down with the kids.....

Anyway, FUD is one that I do know and can believe, *Fear, Uncertainty and Doubt.*

This is basically what every women goes through each time she starts a new *"diet"*.

The fear of gaining more weight!
The uncertainty of the foods allowed!
The doubt that she will achieve her goal!

But wouldn't life be far more joyful and enjoyable if we didn't have this overwhelming negative reaction? Remove the rules, remove the FUD!

But, can we change *FUD* to mean something different? Can we mix this shit up a little bit?
Oh yes! Ladies I give you my very own version of FUD

**Fearlessly
Unstoppable &
Deserving**

Ladies, here is how we roll!

Be fearless in the pursuit of what sets your soul of fire!

A woman becomes unstoppable once she realises she deserves better!

Go out for what you deserve, don't settle!

So that is my take on FUD, make it yours too!

Let go of the rules, throw out the restrictions, dismiss the negative commentary and tear down the false expectations.

Live freely,
Live lovingly,
Live YOUR life!
Live in YOUR BODY!

Haters Gonna Hate

No matter what you do or what you might achieve, you may always feel as though you are being judged.
It's a sad fact that we all spend a great amount of our precious time and energy worrying and fussing over what other people think.

Whether it is what you wear, what you eat, your hair colour/style, being in the gym or just being you.
We are all a little too wrapped up in what complete strangers might think about us.

The fear of others thoughts bears a huge burden and can often go as far as stopping you from doing the things that you most want to do, or living the life that you most want to live.

I have been guilty of this as much as any body, but the moment that I realised and acknowledged this, things changed.

My own fears of others judgements went so far that they actually stopped me from having fun!
And I have missed out on a lot of memories as a result!

You see, I have a fear of deep water, that is no secret, it is a genuine fear.
But my beliefs told me that if I was to go in to the water, if I was to try and swim in the pool whilst on holiday, then there was a very high chance that I would "freak out".
And that would cause everyone around the pool to laugh at me, ridicule me, point at me.. NOTICE ME!

I would be the laughing stock of the entire hotel complex.

For years, I would just sit and watch everybody else jumping in to the pool, riding the water slides, snorkelling and having an absolutely great time.

I desperately wanted to do all of these things, but my fear had grown out of control.
I had turned a fear of deep water into a fear of looking like an idiot.
So, I missed out on all of the fun!

It was only a matter of weeks before I started writing this book that I actually tossed care to one side and overcame this fear... and do you know what, I had a bloody great time!

I didn't freak out!
I didn't drown!
I didn't get laughed at!
But girls, I laughed so much! I laughed from the bottom of my belly and had so much fun!

In honesty, no body really gets through life without being judged, the key is how you deal with it.
Or if you bother acknowledging it at all.

I chose not to acknowledge it, I turned a blind eye! What did the opinion of these people matter anyway, they are all strangers, I'd never see them again, so I chose not to care!

I had the choice! I made that choice! It was my choice!

As Eleanor Roosevelt once said *"Do what you feel in your heart is right - for you'll be criticised anyway. You'll be damned if you do, and damned if you don't"*

And, Aristotle said *"There is only way to avoid criticism, do nothing, say nothing and be nothing"*

I'll be frank here, most people don't really give a damn about what others are doing or saying. Most people are so wrapped up in their own lives and their own worries of judgement.

But their judgement of you, or any other person, is more of a reflection of their own lives, their own insecurities, their own needs.

What matters most is how you feel about yourself.

You need to get over your fears and controls, let go!

Start loving and living! And stop worrying about others opinions.

People who matter wont judge and people who judge don't matter!

Never judge a book by its cover!

Sorority Solidarity

We may not have it all together, but together we have it all!

Come on, we're all girls here, and we all know that sometimes girls can be a little bit bitchy, but wouldn't it be lovely if we could all just get along and be nice?

Now, I am a super friendly person most of the time, but there are odd occasions when I can feel my inner demon trying to resume control (usually *when my guard is down*) and sometimes, the odd thought of hers does escape me.

Ooops! But I am still only human!

I remember being on holiday, and after a few scrummy Pina Coladas, I felt super chilled and pretty great.

I had to *"break the seal"* and whilst in the queue to the ladies I made polite conversation with the lady in front of me, or at least I tried to.

I commented on how lovely her dress was (*which it genuinely was*) and the look that she gave me, well it's the kind of face that you pull when you realise that you have stepped in something quite nasty.

I was a little taken back by this look, but then she proceeded to slam the main door into the toilets in my face as she said "*I am next in the queue!*"

Wow…. erm… I didn't quite know how to process her reaction.

It did cross my mind to swing open the door and yell at her, but what's the point. How "effin" rude of her, but I don't need to go to that level.
Do I!?

Anyway, she pee'd, I pee'd and we never crossed paths again. No bother to me!

But did she really need to be so aggressive?

Of course she didn't, but I think that this was the reaction of a very unhappy person.

Anyway, like I said, wouldn't it be amazing if we could all just be nice?

Smile at the girl on the check out till.
Chat to the lady serving you in the bar.
Be nice to the lady behind you in the queue.

Why is it so difficult?

It all comes back to those pesky judgements really, fuelled by our own insecurities, our own beliefs, our own expectations.
We've judged the book by the cover, made up the story and it will be darn difficult to re-write it now.

Why is it so hard to accept a compliment?
Why can't we let a little love shine it?
Why is it so shocking that someone else thinks you look great?

When someone compliments you, thank them. It's polite!
If you see someone in a gorgeous dress, tell them!
Make her day!

When someone remarks that your hair looks great, say thanks and maybe even recommend your awesome hairdresser.

Share the love with each other.

We all have to share this planet, so make it a nice place to be.

Stop saying things like:

"Oh this old dress…" Come on, we both know that you have never worn it before!

"Urgh, these? Hmmm, they make me look fat" Really? Stop downgrading yourself and fishing for a pick me up compliment.

"Don't be fooled, it's all Make up!" Seriously, come on ladies, just accept that someone else thinks you look kick ass!

We really do need to stop slamming compliments back down, accept them graciously! Be grateful, thankful and appreciate them!

Only the other morning I told one of my clients that she was looking really well. She replied to me with:
"More likely my new moisturiser than me being well"

Actually, I wasn't commenting on her skin, I was thinking how fresh her eyes looked, how awake, how sparkly.

Just learn to let some of that love flood in to your lives and you will begin to feel loved with it.

Accept that you are worthy of compliments, and stop downgrading them.

Accept that you are beautiful and appreciate the love.

When you finally let go of the rules and see all of this love, your life will change, as will your attitude and your relationship with yourself.

Us girls need to stick together, that's why I created the social media groups, so we can all share love and light with each other, make sure you come and join us by the way.

Love yourself and allow others to love you too!

Feelings Don't Lie

I talked in earlier chapters about your goals, finding the emotional connection with them and "feeling" the emotions of your future self.

Something that I didn't mention however, was measuring your achievements and your results.

As a personal trainer, I was always told to focus on numbers, weight, inches, percentages. But as I transitioned into nutrition and lifestyle coaching, I quickly realised that this kind of measuring just wasn't going to work.

It sets rules and restrictions, which although may not be directly associated with eating or dieting, the outcome would still become one of expectation, disappointment, guilt and negative energy.

So how should you measure achievements?

Rather than focussing on what the scales tell you, start to focus on how you are feeling.

In fact, I urge you to break up completely with the scales, throw them out.
You no longer need this kind of restrictive guidance tool in your life.
You want to live free, so break free.

If you have tried to live a "healthier" lifestyle before, dieted, worked out, or whatever methods you have used, what was the first thing that you noticed changing?

Was it weight, inches, dress size or was it how you felt?

It is ALWAYS based on feeling.

If you lost weight you felt proud. If you lost inches you felt motivated, if you changed a dress size you felt accomplished.
But, really, it's all just about feeling.
It's all measured by how you feel.

- Happier
- Stronger
- Empowered
- Enlightened
- Uplifted
- Proud
- Energetic
- Alive
- Awake
- Fulfilled
- Powerful
- Loved
- Important

How do you FEEL?

I have spoken many times during this book about paying attention, listening and hearing... So listen!

Eat the foods that make you feel. Or more specifically eat the foods that make you feel how you WANT to feel!

Listen to how foods make you feel.
Learn what your body loves and feed more love into her.

Imagine spending every day of the rest of your life filling your body with love.
How do you want to feel today?

Consider my earlier point as well, rather than focusing on what you do want, think about what you don't want. Go opposite!

How do you NOT want to feel?

Which foods make your feel sluggish, slow and lethargic?
Which foods cause you to feel bloated, sick or constipated?
Which foods increase your period pains? (yes food can do that)
Which foods cause you to suffer headaches?
Which foods make you feel guilt?

OR...

Which foods make you feel strong?
Which foods make you feel empowered?
Which foods make you feel like you are supporting your future self?
Which foods give you a good boost?
Which foods are fun?

Ask, notice, learn.

Let food be thy medicine and let your feelings guide and determine your food.

Whilst we are talking about feelings, you don't need a Monday to start feeling.

You don't need to wait until the new year or after easter.
You don't need to wait until after the summer holidays or until the kids go back to school.
And you don't need to wait for permission from any body else.

Just start feeling, right now!
Right in this moment, ask yourself - How do I feel?

How do I WANT to feel?

Let your feelings truly guide you to freedom.
Freedom from rules, restrictions, deadlines or anything else.

Just Feel! Right now!

Remember EVERY feeling that you have, is your body trying to communicate something to you.

Feel if she is full or if she has had enough.
Feel if you could chew slower, savour food and help your body digest better.
Feel if you could stop eating just before you reach full.

Your body is talking to you, all you have to do is feel!

The first duty of love is to listen.

Paul Tillich

Food-ism

How much would you love to eat whatever the hell you wanted?

I had so many rules for so long… I can have this, but not that, if I want this then I cant have that, I do want that, but should really have this.

Oh Bugger off! Seriously!

I eat whatever the fuck I want!!!
That is my only rule these days.

If I want a bar of chocolate, I have it!
If I want to eat take away, I have it!
If I want some ice cream, I have it! (*as long as it is goats milk, as I am allergic to cows milk!*)

No rules means NO RULES!

It all really just boils down to what you want!

Not what you think you want, or what clever marketing campaigns make you think you want.
It's not about what friends, family members or society expects you to want.
It is just about what YOU want!

But, unlike the opinions of many, just because you eat whatever you want, doesn't mean that you are delving head first into a take away or chocolate sponge cake every night.

You see, if you want to feel good, if you want to feel awesome, then you just have to eat for this feeling.

Put it this way, today is Monday, it's a hot today (*about 31degrees, who knew the UK got this warm*) and I am sat in my garden office writing these words, as I think back over the weekend and what I chose to eat, well, it went a bit like this:

For breakfast on Saturday I had tomatoes, feta cheese and cucumber on crisp breads with olive oil and salad herbs.
Then for lunch, I had a grilled halloumi sandwich on ciabatta bread with tomatoes and guacamole.
For dinner, my partner and I went to the pub and I had a spicy chickpea veggie burger, with a surf a turf share platter, washed down with a few beers and a Gin & Tonic.

I felt good on Sunday, and carried on the awesomeness with a spicy quinoa and rice breakfast, lunch was a coronation chicken sandwich on a granary role and piri piri chicken for dinner.

Guess what, I enjoyed all of my meals and felt awesome as a result.
And today, Monday, I am still feeling great because I chose my foods and meals based on
a) what I wanted and like and
b) how I want to feel.

_____

On the whole, we all need more nutrient dense foods in our bodies, most people have no idea just how good they could feel, because their body has never been given the nourishment or fed with love.

You just need to trust that your body will tell you the right message, that your body will tell you exactly what she wants and needs to feel great.

We need to trust that our body wants real food, real goodness and not cheap man-made imitations.

As I have already said, it's not about being perfect, there really is no such things, it's about letting go, giving love and receiving love in return.

Food is a pleasure and if you let more of it into your life and into your body, you will begin to see that food really is amazing.

And remember, if you do choose to eat something that is not serving the future you, that's ok too!

Just own it!

Don't fall for food-ism!

Break the rules more often and you will gain a huge advantage over those too afraid to risk it.

F#!K RULES

Break free from all of the jaded shackles,
Allow your life to breathe and flow.
Stand up to all of life biggest tackles,
Let your true self thrive and glow.

Rules are there for the breaking,
Not to live your life by.
This is your future self in the making,
Sit up and hear your body cry.

Let food be thy saviour,
Let love guide you on your path.
Open your heart to all of the flavours,
And allow yourself to laugh.

You are strong and beautiful and worthy,
You deserve the best in life.
Don't spend your time being so nervy,
Live for today without the strife.

I know that you can do this,
I am giving you all of the tools,
To go live from today in utter bliss,
Because you stood up and said F#!k Rules!

Forgive & Forget

We all waste so much time and energy worrying about food, just think of all of the things that you could be doing with that time.
If you could just take responsibility, accountability, ownership, and just move on, without worry?
Remember how I said Maria brought some muffins in, you had a muffin, you enjoyed it….. this acceptance of food needs to start happening. Today!

I have said so many times through the course of this book that you just need to accept your choices, without feeling guilt, anxiety or self judgement.

Just take ownership, be accountable!
It is YOUR choice!

You are the queen of your destiny, the ruler of your thoughts.

If you choose to have something, have it, taste it, enjoy it.
Take your time with it!
Saviour it!
Once you have finished, just carry on as usual, don't dwell, don't get frustrated, don't get angry, just get over it!
A bump in the road does not signal the end of the journey! And to be honest, it isn't even a bump in the road!

Don't try to undo it!
Don't try to make a mends for it!
Don't even try to make up for it!
Just carry on!

Take responsibility for your choices and your actions, and be aware of them.
No one else has made you do it... It was your choice!

Just by becoming more accountable, you will automatically start to think more about your choices, and make more supportive ones as you do.

When you forgive you heal.
When you let go, you grow.

Find Passion in the Pans

Not everyone loves spending time in the kitchen cooking, and honestly, I am one of these people.
Well, that's not strictly true, I use to love cooking, and would always cook for my mum after my dad passed away.

I use to make some really yummy things like Swordfish kebabs and vegetable pizza (*I even made the dough*).
I would make sugar free shortbread biscuits and my piece de la resistance was my mango cheesecake, and my tiramisu.

But once I had a full time job, a full time relationship, and I had moved out of my mothers house, despite desperately trying I just couldn't keep this passion in the pans going.
It soon became a thwarted love/hate relationship with jars of pre-made sauces and tins of anything I could get my hands on.
I had fully disconnected!

I lost my way in the kitchen, until one day I found myself with this huge Aga oven with seven hobs and two ovens. Wow, I remember being so excited about cooking with that oven.
I would wake up in the middle of the night and just make a lasagne, or a pie, or some bread just for the hell of it.

I found that sparkle & love for food again.... Until, I moved out of that house and had to leave the ridiculously amazing Aga behind. I was gutted!

I have dabbled with my cooking passions since, but for so many years, I have worked late into the evening training clients.

So my partner assumed most of the cooking responsibilities, but that doesn't stop me from experimenting with flavours and creating my own recipes.

Recipes that you can find on my blog or facebook page, shared for all to try. You're welcome!

But many of the women that I speak to have also lost their sparkle in the kitchen, not necessarily because they no longer enjoy making food, but because they struggle to find the energy, the oomph, the inspiration, the passion to get in there and play.

With many of the women that I have worked with, when we have investigated the problem, it usually turns out that their kitchen just isn't really that hospitable.

There is lots of stuff laying around, things piled up, unused recipe books staring at them, judging them. Fruits in the fruit bowl that have been then longer than I care to know.

And then, there is all of these weird and wonderful new foods that we have available to us now, foods that we just have no clue how to prepare, cook or serve.

There are foods that you can use in a main meal as a rice substitute, that you can also use as a breakfast alternative, I mean... how does that even work?

I have spent years trying to create recipes that are fun, interesting, easy and reasonably quick.

Recipes that the whole family can enjoy and share together.

Recipes that can be batch cooked and frozen for use throughout the week, to save time.

The biggest thing I have found with all of the women that I speak to, is that there needs to be passion in the pans.
Food is an emotional, sensory thing and you need to enjoy it, love it, put love into it and get love back out of it.

And we need to start by clearing up our kitchens.

Have a good old clear out of the old rusty tins of chicken soup, throw out anything that is out of date, past its best or let's be honest, never going to be eaten!

Clear out the food that you do not want in your home, let alone in your body.

And start fresh, and literally I mean fresh.

Fill your kitchen with fresh herb plants that fill the room with a delicious smell, whilst adding a little greenery and colour to the room.

Fill your fruit bowl with colours and textures that everyone can enjoy, make it look pretty. But make sure that they will get eaten or used!
Don't waste food!

Fill your fridge with wholesome, whole foods that you know how to prepare, that you want to eat and enjoy.

Start simple!
Pick out one or two new recipes to try each week, and plan them in to a day when you can take your time.

Put love into your meals.

If you want to try playing with a food that you are not sure how to prepare, do a quick internet search and see how to prep and cook with it before you buy it.

Find out if it is going to take you loads of time and effort? Is it going to be too much for you to deal with time wise? Be honest with yourself. Don't bite off more than you can chew.

My absolute golden tip for finding love in cooking is to be playful. Literally do what your parents always told you not to do... Play with your food!

Make it fun, inviting, exciting, interesting and enjoyable. Make it sensory!

Here is a few more tips for adding your sparkle to your meals:

- Cook with Coconut Oil or Extra Virgin Olive Oil.
- Make more than you need so you can freeze left overs for lunch or another dinner.
- Spend some time making your kitchen friendly, welcoming and light.
- Have everything you need close by, use large mason jars for counter top storage and get the kids to decorate the jars if you like.
- Allow enough time to prep your food, or pre-prep a few days before. Try not to feel rushed or bogged down.
- Ask the family if they want to get involved with cooking, and make it a family-time thing. This will help children learn about food and cooking too. What a great example to set!

- Look up some great "treat" recipes, like my Greek Yoghurt Rainbow Bites. Keep things fun and light hearted.
- Listen to your favourite music, podcast or radio show whilst cooking, dance, wiggle, smile, sing.
- Experiment and taste as your cook, add herbs, flavours and textures to your meals as you go, play!

Put love into your food, so that the food can return the love to you and your body.

Make your kitchen the fun place in the house to be, the place where the real magic happens.

Enjoy cooking and find love in the ladles.

The secret ingredient is always love.

Give Yourself A Hug

The relationship that you have with yourself, is truly a remarkable one, and the most important of all of the relationships that you will ever have.

You and your body are in this together for a lifetime. Whatever you experience, your body experiences with you.

But we rarely spare a thought for this beautiful and miraculous relationship, we hardly ever see it, recognise it, acknowledge it or care for it.
We are all too busy building other relationships, trying to make things work with other people.

But if our relationship with ourselves was healthier, love-filled, nurturing, then all of these other relationships wouldn't need quite so much effort.

Without the relationship that you have with your body, none of these other precious relationships would even be possible, remember, how much do you need your body?

Spend a moment just thinking about all of the relationships that you have had in your life so far, which stand out?

Which is your warmest, fuzziest friendship?
Which would you do anything to protect?
Which makes you feel loved?
Which offers you sanctuary, safety and security?
Which gives you the most in return?

We all have one relationship that we cherish, but is it the relationship you have with yourself?

What qualities would you look for in a partner?
What would make that relationship shine like no other?

Which of these qualities are present in your relationship with yourself?

Every choice, action, reaction, friend, feeling, emotion, relationship, moment and thing is a true reflection of your relationship with yourself.

We attract what we are!
We treat how we want to be treated!
We behave how we want to be behaved around!

Everything is a direct reflection and result of your own relationship with yourself, your body and your mind.

If you want more love, then you need to put more love in.

Be your own reason to look forward to tomorrow, and whoever you invite into your life will feel the same way.

To fall in love with yourself is the first secret to happiness

Let Love Light The Way

You may have seen those images on social media, or seen an article from a personal trainer or coach saying:

70% nutrition, 30% exercise.

As much as there is truth in this statement, nothing will work if your headspace is not in the right place.

Mindset is one of the most neglected aspects of transformations in the health and fitness industry, and in truth, all personal trainers would benefit from studying mindset, mindfulness, psychology and so on.

The human mind is a deep and mysterious place, and if I had never invested my time in learning about the goings on of the human thought process, well I would likely still be in a very dark and lonely place.

Opening up your mind to yourself, and your heart to love of yourself is fundamentally the key to everything else in life, happiness, confidence, contentment, relaxation, peace, self respect, self love, acceptance, forgiveness, and freedom to name just a few.

That day in London, staring in the mirror, reciting words to myself, the discomfort I felt was tangible.
The pain I could feel bubbling, the hurts, the old wounds, the never forgiving myself, the never appreciating myself all came to the surface, and it hurt. It hurt a lot.
But it opened my eyes.

I saw a light that offered me resolution, peace, happiness, and I had to start walking that path before I self destructed.

My mentor that day, pushed me, harder than anyone had ever pushed me before and she was feeling my pain with me.
She was seeing my pain manifest as tears in my eyes and rolling down my cheeks, as I realised all of the hurt I had been bottling up, keeping locked in. I was ready to blow.
In fact, looking back on that day, the other people attending the course, I don't think there was one person who didn't cry, and there were some big old burly body builders in that room.

Seeing all of this hurt in me, allowed me to see what I needed to do. How I needed to accept that I was hurting myself, self harming in an emotional way.
My coping mechanism were flawed and failing me massively.

I knew the direction I needed to travel in and I followed my heart, rather than my head.
In that moment, in that acceptance of heart over head, I changed my life.
I changed everything about me, my relationship, my lifestyle.

Arriving home from London after the three days, my partner of 8 years said *"you're acting different!"*

But that didn't change how I felt.

I knew that I needed to do this for me, for my own health, sanity, happiness and future.

Opening my heart to myself has been a huge journey.

A journey that will never end, because I am always learning, discovering, practising, praising, appreciating. I am always growing inside, and with it grows my energy, my love, my self respect.

I don't make demands of my body anymore, I just listen, I respect and I nurture.
And I smile!

Look at yourself in the mirror and speak to yourself, look deep into your own eyes and apologise.

Apologise for all of the hurt, pain, neglect, abuse. Apologise for never listening, and promise to listen more from now on.
Forgive for anything in the past, whatever you have done or not done, you are worthy of love.
Tell yourself, I'm sorry, I forgive you, you're worth it, I love you!

Keep affirming your new openness, love and care to your body. Keep opening your heart more and more to her.
Give back and come home to your body.
Show love, Give love, receive love.

Ask questions and wait for the answers.

Be loyal, be generous, be loving, be compassionate.

Love and respect your body in a way that makes you want to look after it, that makes you want to nurture it, that makes you want to love it.

Make your choices match how you want to feel.

Sit up, forgive, love, pay attention and be at one with your body.

Let love light your path and lead you in the right direction.

There is no limit to what can be achieved when you let love lead the way.

Your Dream Body

We all have a *"dream body"* pictured in our mind, but is it actually your dream, or just what you believe to be perfection?

As I have already said there is no such thing, perfection becomes obsession and there is no end to that journey. No happy end may I add.

A lot of women have told me that they would love to have the body of an A-List Hollywood actress, but when you consider that this actress has a totally different body shape and body type to my client, how likely is it that she can achieve that?

If I am honest, I really do not enjoy bursting bubbles, I really don't, but to set a goal based on someone else reality, is often a shortcut to disappointment.

Instead of focusing on that someone else has already achieved, focus on what would truly make you happy. Don't settle for less though.

If I gave you a magic pen and piece of paper that could capture the image in your mind, how would you look? What would your dream body look like?

Remember how we visualised the future you earlier in the book, bring that image of you back into mind, see her now.

I want you to think about a scenario that you would love to feel comfortable and confident in.

It could be wearing one of the low slung backless summer dresses we spoke about, going out for a glammed up night with the girls.

Perhaps wearing some swimwear on the beach without a cover up, is it a bikini, a tankini, an all in one? How does it look?

Or maybe, you are just chilling with your friends and family, wearing some skinny jeans and a casual top, just looking awesome and feel amazing.

How does your body look?
How do you feel in your body?
How can you make this body yours?
What can you do right now to take just one step closer?

Don't waste your time and precious energy obsessing about how some celebrity looks, think about you, your body, your future!

Picture your body, take a mental snapshot.

Write down all of the words that describe your future body and how it makes you feel.

Build this body in your mind based on you and your own personal dreams, no one else's.

Then allow this dream body, this confident, gorgeous, beautiful, strong, amazing woman, this future you, allow her to guide your choices and decisions today, tomorrow and the next day.

Allow the future you to come to life within you today!

If you behave like you are already that person, then that person is who you will become.

You are creating your own future as we speak.

As I have said a gazillion times over the pages of this book, choose actions that support the future you.

Choose your Future!
Choose your happiness!
Choose YOU!

And I said to my body, softly,
"I want to be your friend"
It took a long breath and
replied "I have been waiting my
whole life for this."

Nayyirah Waheed

The Spiritual Sanctity of Self Love

I chose the energy of the universe to help me on my way to self love, empowerment and happiness, but you do not have to follow me.
As I established earlier, what has worked for one may not be the right choice for another.

But, it is **YOUR** choice!
It is your right to choose how you go about healing and finding love.

Reiki, crystals, meditation have all served me in making a much deeper connection with my body that goes way beyond hearing what food she is asking for, or if I need to slow down.
It has tuned me in to my life goals, my femininity , my ambition, my love, my aura, and energy.
It has guided me in healing past hurts, making a mends and forgiving myself for things that I have done in the past.

It has shown me if, and when I am on the right path, and where I may need to spend some more time and focus in my life.
It has allowed me to live in peace, no longer fighting with my own mind.

All of these things have led to a much greater friendship with my body, and achieving this love has opened up my relationships with others to give and receive love more willingly.

All of these changes have brought me more happiness, more excitement and an even brighter future.

Reiki may not be for you, but if you can tune in to your body enough, she will tell you the right path to take.

Whether it is holistic, spiritual healing, coaching, guidance, self taught, group coaching or something entirely different, whichever route you take, I want you to know that I am here for you if you need any kind of support or help.

My online group will be there for you 24/7, as well as my online courses.

My blog, my website and my social media accounts are there whenever you need a pep, and so too are all of my amazing followers and clients.

Us girls gotta stick together.

Only Do It If You Love It!

You may find it strange that we have almost reached the end of this book all about transforming your relationship with your body and food, yet still, especially as I am a personal trainer, I haven't mentioned anything about "exercise".

And here is why:

It doesn't matter what you do, as long as you love it.

Whether it's walking, running, dancing, skipping, weight lifting, fitness classes, swimming, line dancing, trampolining, yoga, tai chi, hoovering or anything else, movement will come naturally, you just gotta do what you love!

As your love for your body grows, along with your mind and your food, you will start to love movement as well.

Just stop thinking of "exercise" as "exercise", it is just movement.

Allow your body to move naturally at your own pace, and when you want to, and good things will come.

Don't try and burn yourself out, over do it or injure yourself.
Don't try to bite off more than you can chew and try something that is beyond your level of fitness.
And STOP thinking about what any body else might think.

Embrace Yourself

To finish, I want to encourage you to embrace yourself.

Embrace who you truly are and what makes you truly happy.

Embrace your today and your tomorrow, and see that you are worthy of love.

Embrace your choices, take ownership and enjoy the journey that you have made, or are about to make.

Embrace every chance, opportunity and moment to be the future you.

Embrace your imperfections as perfections, love every inch of your mind, body and soul.

Embrace those around you who love, cherish and support you.

Embrace all of the other woman who, like you, are giving it their best damn shot.

Embrace your life and everything in it.

Embrace your Body!
Embrace your Mind!
Embrace YOU!

Never apologise for being a strong and powerful fucking woman!

Lesley works with women all over the world, empowering them and encouraging them to love themselves for who they truly are.

No woman should ever feel alone!

Lesley has launched numerous online programmes, courses and groups to support like-minded women who want to find love for themselves and feel amazing in their own skin.

If you would like to find out more about working with Lesley, then visit the website or contact her directly using the details below.

Beyond Nutrition and Mindset coaching, Lesley is also a qualified Usui Reiki Master, and can perform distance and group healings. If you choose to use spiritual and universal guidance to connect with your soul, contact Lesley to discuss the distance reiki services.

Come and join the online community on Facebook:
https://www.facebook.com/groups/LMCoaching/

Visit the website:
www.lmfitness.info

And talk to Lesley directly at:
lesley@lmfitness.info

To all of the beautiful and amazing women!

Thank you for taking the time to read my little book. I hope that you have found some truly inspirational and magical information that you can make use of whilst building your relationship and creating your future.

There is no right or wrong way to find love for yourself, and if anyone tells you differently, then please remember what I said about the diet & food industries, and their marketing tactics.

During the course of this book, I haven't told you want to do, I have merely planted little heart shaped seeds in your mind, and I really do hope that you water them enough to grow a beautiful, big, blossoming relationship with yourself.

You are amazing!
You are my inspiration!
You make my life so fulfilling!
And for that, I thank you all!

I am honoured that you chose to pick up this book, and am humbled that you have read it this far.

As a thank you, I would like to offer you the opportunity to come and work through a "You-Nique" call with me, whenever you are ready. Just follow the link below, and request a session.

And ladies, beautiful, wonderful, gorgeous, strong ladies, please come and join me in my online community.
I am regularly online doing live videos, Q&A's, webinars and more, and I would love for you to join me.

From the deepest and happiest place within my heart, thank you!

Much, much love and all the very best,

Lesley :)

xxx

Request your You-Nique Call:
www.lmfitness.info/you-re-you-nique/

33534544R00130

Printed in Great Britain
by Amazon